ST. PAUL

AND

SOCIAL PSYCHOLOGY

An Introduction

to the Epistle to the Ephesians

BY

F. R. BARRY, M.A., D.S.O.

PRINCIPAL OF THE ORDINATION TEST SCHOOL, KNUTSFORD

HUMPHREY MILFORD
OXFORD UNIVERSITY PRESS
LONDON EDINBURGH GLASGOW COPENHAGEN
NEW YORK TORONTO MELBOURNE CAPE TOWN
BOMBAY CALCUTTA MADRAS SHANGHAI
1923

PRINTED IN ENGLAND
AT THE OXFORD UNIVERSITY PRESS
BY FREDERICK HALL

PREFACE

THIS little book is best explained by its origin. It has been my habit for nearly four years at Knutsford to meet the School for half an hour each morning, before the ordinary lectures began, to read and explain the Bible with them. In this way we have covered together nearly the whole of the New Testament and certain portions of the Old. In Lent 1921 we read *Ephesians*, and this book is more or less the result. I used no notes for these talks and kept no record; but on this occasion a diligent hearer took down a summary of what I said, out of which the chapters that follow have been worked up. They are thus intended rather to suggest a general line of approach to *Ephesians* than to take the place of a detailed commentary—a task which would be quite beyond my powers. But such as it is, this book is an attempt to expound St. Paul's thought in relation to modern needs and the modern outlook. It is also intended as a contribution towards the revival of Christo-centric Churchmanship. That is to say, the writer accepts the values of that 'catholic' conception of Christianity as membership in a visible, sacramental Society of which this Epistle is the highest expression. But simultaneously he tries to purge it of a tendency to mere ecclesiasticism by pressing back to the New Testament with its uncompromising emphasis on the centrality of Jesus Christ. I have not discussed the Epistle exhaustively. In particular, I have said very little about St. Paul's mystical experience. But

I have tried to envisage the Body of Christ as a vivid fact in the actual world of to-day. It is sought to show that the Christian Society, conceived as (it is argued) St. Paul conceived it and as its Founder willed it to be, supplies the only effective solution for national and international problems. And this is considered closely in relation to current tendencies in History and the new science of Social Psychology, as well as the facts of contemporary politics, with a special reference to the League of Nations. It is argued both that Christian thought must take more account of Social Psychology and that the latter can only really avail if brought into closer connexion with Christian thought.

It would probably have been a better book, and certainly would have been easier to follow, if it could have been considerably longer. But I have to accept the conditions of my work. I can only write under the greatest difficulties. I have to be content with odd half-hours, often separated by several weeks; and no consistent, closely reasoned treatise can possibly be produced in such a way. So I had to choose between publishing in this form and not publishing at all. It is not for the author to feel confident that the right alternative has been chosen. Yet there were several things that I wanted to say, even if I had to say them clumsily.

Most of the book follows familiar lines; it is only in Chapters V, VI, and VII that I should claim to have made anything approximating to an attempt at an original contribution. My first attempt at developing the ideas which are now suggested in Chapter VI was in a University Sermon at Cambridge, which was subsequently published in the *Interpreter*.

The book was originally intended to form one of the series called ‘ The Church's Message for the coming time ’, for which (I am ashamed to say) it was promised as long ago as 1915. But for several reasons when it was at last written it seemed better to publish it independently. My thanks are due to the Editor of that series, the Rev. H. T. Knight, for his generous acquiescence in this arrangement.

Like every one else, I owe much to the help of friends too numerous to mention by name. Probably very little here is my own, though I have acknowledged such debts as I can trace. My devoted Secretary, Mr. A. W. Hooper, now a tutor at the Test School, made the book possible at all by taking down a record of what was said. And I must express my thanks to my former colleague, Mr. J. L. Etty, Warden of Wantage Hall, Reading, for cutting his way through my manuscript and turning some of the sentences into English. I have also received some very useful suggestions from the reader at the Oxford Press.

I hope this small book may not be wholly useless. In any case I have enjoyed writing it as a reminder of many of my friends at Knutsford and of happy years spent together with them.

KNUTSFORD. F. R. B.
December 1922.

CONTENTS

Blessed *be* the God and Father of our Lord Jesus Christ, who hath blessed us with every spiritual blessing in the heavenly *places* in Christ: even as he chose us in him before the foundation of the world, that we should be holy and without blemish before him in love: having foreordained us unto adoption as sons through Jesus Christ unto himself, according to the good pleasure of his will, to the praise of the glory of his grace, which he freely bestowed on us in the Beloved: in whom we have our redemption through his blood, the forgiveness of our trespasses, according to the riches of his grace, which he made to abound toward us.—Eph. i. 3–8.

This I say therefore, and testify in the Lord, that ye no longer walk as the Gentiles also walk, in the vanity of their mind, being darkened in their understanding, alienated from the life of God because of the ignorance that is in them, because of the hardening of their heart; who being past feeling gave themselves up to lasciviousness, to make a trade of all uncleanness with greediness. But ye did not so learn Christ; if so be that ye heard him, and were taught in him, even as truth is in Jesus: that ye put away, as concerning your former manner of life, the old man, which waxeth corrupt after the lusts of deceit; and that ye be renewed in the spirit of your mind, and put on the new man, which after God hath been created in righteousness and holiness of truth.—Eph. iv. 17–24.

CHAPTER I

THE PROBLEM OF CIVILIZATION

That ye may know what is the hope of his calling . . . and what the exceeding greatness of his power.'—Eph. i. 18, 19.

THE world into which Christianity first came was extraordinarily like our own. The more we know of the conditions—political, psychological, religious—of the first century of the Roman Empire, the more striking grows the parallel between them and those in which we live. The background of the apostolic age, across which the New Testament characters move, might almost seem to be the twentieth century. Its broad outlines are familiar enough, but they may perhaps be roughly sketched in here; for nothing is likely to give a clearer conception of the vividness and reality of the Gospel than to see it in its concrete setting amid the life and problems of those days. To understand what the Gospel means to us, we must know what it meant to those who first received it. To say that Christianity is universal, not limited to one age or generation, does not imply that it is vague and nebulous with no definition and no historical context. It is universal just because it satisfies the particular needs and problems of each generation. If we want to know what it really says and does that can avail to save the world to-day, it is best to ask what it really said and did in a closely similar situation. Then we can tell what it has to say to us.

Like ours, the world into which the new faith came was crushing men by its complexity. It was a war-weary world, baffled in its attempts at reconstruction, dazed by vast and bewildering transitions. Established social conditions were collapsing. Accepted class-distinctions had grown blurred; the profiteer was entering into society and the unprivileged were beginning to count. The old regime could no longer be taken for granted. Political groupings were shifting and breaking up, old ties and loyalties were being snapped, and the individual was left spiritually homeless and self-conscious in a cosmopolitan civilization. Externally brilliant, it was morally rotten, and wealth and elegance scarcely drew a veil over cruelty and decadent forms of vice, of which the Epistles give relentless catalogues. There is, of course, a bright side to the picture. Noble aspirations were there in plenty, fine idealisms, kindness, courtesy; only, there was no moral driving-power. The distinctive note of the imperial world is the note of disillusionment. Men longed for a fresh start which they could not get, for a deliverance they could not find, for a fellowship which they could not achieve. They could not recover because they had not hope. People were lost and lonely and disappointed. There was no vital faith in anything to simplify life for them and make it whole and liberate their moral energies. For the old religions had been undermined, and few believed them any longer. The great majority of people fought through a fog of choking superstitions, credulous, magical, and demon-haunted. Some found in the Greek and Eastern 'Mysteries', with their thrilling sacramental worship, some form of at least emotional relief. A surprising number were hangers-on of Judaism, as a moral but not a ceremonial code.[1] The traditional priesthoods had become a farce: the real religious guides were the philosophers, especially those of the Stoic school, of whom Seneca (Nero's tutor and the brother of Gallio) is the best known. The professors of philosophy were almost spiritual 'directors', at any rate to the cultured, leisured classes. But Stoicism offered good advice, and the heart of the world was aching for redemption.

It is true, of course, that Our Lord's life and teaching moved within far narrower boundaries. The Gospel which was to renew the world was preached in primitive Galilean villages in a simple and little-organized

[1] These are the 'God-fearers' of Acts x. 2, 22, xiii. 16, &c. See K. Lake, *Earlier Epistles of St. Paul*, pp. 37 ff. The number of Jews in the Empire is estimated at about 4 to 4½ million out of 54 million, i.e. roughly, 8⅓ per cent. of the whole population. Beloch's estimates quoted in Harnack, *Mission and Expansion*, vol. i, chap. i.

society. But it was on the ampler stage of civilization in the Graeco-Roman cities that its implications were worked out. In the complex life of the early Empire its experiments were made and its experiences verified. Those who tell us that a social ethic preached to an agricultural population in Galilee and the Syrian country-side can have no adequate solution for our Industrial Democracies, may fairly be asked to read the actual records. The earliest Church was obsessed by no such scruples.[1] After a momentary hesitation it turned at once to the world of Imperial culture to lay the foundations of a new civilization. Within a few years after the Crucifixion, Palestine was already a backwater. The Christian mission went to the urban life of the great seaports and economic capitals, to work the Gospel out in action. The whole civilized world was represented when, six weeks after the Resurrection, the Church received its Pentecostal baptism. Within twenty years of the death of Stephen it was charged with 'turning the Empire upside-down' (Acts xvii. 6). It is plain at least that the earliest disciples, who had known the Great Reformer best, did not doubt that His religion could restore and rebuild civilization under conditions far more complex than any that had ever crossed their minds. It was not in Galilee at all, but in Corinth and Ephesus that their work was done. They never supposed they could only appeal to fishermen. As well contend that Meleager of Gadara, author of some of the loveliest Greek elegies, could only have written odes to Gadarene swine! The Greeks said the new faith was 'bad philosophy', and the Jews that it 'offended their moral sense' (1 Cor. i. 23): but nobody said that because it came from Galilee it could have no message for Roman millionaires.

It is doubtless true that the first generation lived their lives under the urgent sense of an imminent Return of Christ, and the sudden, catastrophic rolling-up of the

[1] The issue between St. Paul and his opponents was not whether the Gentile world could be Christianized: that was decided in the Cornelius incident—Acts x and xi. The disputed point was on what terms and with what ceremonial requirements, whether by way of circumcision or not.

civilization of 'the World'. Full allowance must be made for this, and it must be frankly admitted that this belief, falsified as it was by events, impressed on some of the thought of the New Testament a sense which we cannot now accept literally. But it is very easily exaggerated. St. Paul himself finally discarded it, moving from *Thessalonians* to *Ephesians* in his interpretation of Christ's teaching, as St. John advanced from the Synoptic Gospels to the doctrine of Eternal Life in Christ. The latter represents his mature experience. And in any case, however prominent the idea of a 'Coming in the clouds of Heaven' may have been in the minds of the earliest believers, it did *not* work out in the way that is often suggested. It did not paralyse their moral enterprise. They did not say, 'There is no time to change things.' Rather, they said, 'He may come at any moment: Let us get the house ready for Him' (cf. Luke xii. 34 ff.). It sent them out with a passion to save society, and it gave them a certainty in the Eternal world, directing their activity in this. The cruder form of the earlier expectation was soon transmuted into the conviction that supernatural forces were at work destined to overthrow the established order, that Christ was sovereign over human life and at work within human nature through His Present Spirit, lifting it up to a more than earthly destiny. That was a world-overcoming faith. The dominant note of the New Testament is the sense of limitless human possibilities in the transforming power of the Spirit of Christ. That is the basis of all 'Reconstruction'. This faith in human possibilities penetrates all our conceptions of social justice and the Christian organization of Society, and lies at the root of any vivid belief in the renewal of the coming age.

The worst of it is that we Christians as a whole have almost lost any real expectancy. We do not think that Christianity can redeem and change society: we think of it as a means of 'saving souls'. When it was openly stated in 1914 that Christianity had no application to social and political morality, the English Christian conscience was affronted. We went to war to prove that it was not true. Yet it was only stripping the disguise from what, in fact, was too nearly our own attitude. We regarded our religion as mainly concerned with the individual's soul, saving people out of this 'naughty world' rather than making the naughty world a place fit for sons and daughters of God to live in. We did not think it would turn the world upside down. Sometimes the evil in the world was regarded as inevitable, even acquiesced in as a means for exercising 'Christian charity' and training ourselves for Heaven after death. But, says Dean Inge, 'If you once give your moral assent to other people's sins and sorrows as affording a field for your altruistic activities, your moral sense must be in a sadly diseased condition.' It would, no doubt, be a cruel caricature to suggest that this is a normal Christian attitude. Yet it is undeniable that 'soul-culture', or at least salvation for the individual, had become the dominant note of our religion. Christianity had got confused with pietism. There is scarcely a collect in the Anglican Prayer-book with any sense of an adventurous service in the restoration of the world. The request of nearly all of them is 'safety'. The countless manuals of devotion concentrate a great deal too much attention on a debilitating introspectiveness. The monstrous wrongs of the world are left unrecognized, the idea of *corporate* guilt and responsibility sacrificed to personal 'growth in holiness'. It is even sometimes taught that 'resignation' is an advanced stage of Christian virtue, and acceptance of things as they are is miscalled 'obedience to the will of God'. But our Lord said that it is disobedience: 'it is NOT the will of your Father who is in Heaven that one of these little ones should perish.' The need for us all to-day is to remember that Christianity is, from its first beginnings, a revolutionary faith.

Our despairing acquiescence would have been entirely inconceivable to Our Lord's first followers. The Kingdom of God which He preached in Galilee is, through and through, a social salvation. He wanted to rebuild society from its spiritual foundations upwards round the new controlling principle of the true Reality of God. He would be satisfied with nothing less. Religion, for Him, means *doing the will of God*, and He knew that the will of God is health and justice, joy and liberty and brotherhood. He was the supreme Believer in God, and as such the supreme Believer in Mankind. He knew that what was chiefly wrong with the world was a wrong idea about God. He went about awakening in men a new sense of expectancy based upon a renewed belief in God. 'How little you trust God' He used to say. For Him, faith in God carried with it, as inherent in its very nature, a certainty of God's victoriousness. 'All things are possible with God.' His will, because it is His will, must prevail. The Kingdom, because it is God's, must surely come. 'It is His good pleasure to give you the Kingdom.' Therefore Our Lord could move about among men calling them back to a joyous confidence in the availability of God. Thus His ministry was, as a later writer put it, the 'bringing in of a better hope'. He gave back hope to a despairing world, because He brought it face to face with God.

On the foundation of this triumphant certainty He fashioned the new fabric of Society. In His own words, He 'despaired of nobody' (Luke vi. 35, R.V. marg.). He knew that no human life, however broken, was too hard a problem for His Father. He knew that God can give 'new lives for old': that there is a creative love at work in the world, inexhaustible and unfailing, if men would only open their hearts and take it. Thus, however dark the situation, however great the failure and the ruin of the lives with which He was confronted, we can see no trace of Him ever losing heart. He staked all on God's renewing power, and died to prove that His confidence was justified.

There is little in our contemporary Christianity comparable to this massive faith of Jesus. We cannot lead the world until we recover it. 'Is it not clear that one great reason why faith in the Incarnation, the work of Christ and the gift of the Spirit, mean so little to the youth of the nation is that they do not know that the essence of the Christian life is faith, hope, and love?'[1] So we are

[1] *The Army and Religion*, p. 434.

told that Religion is out of touch with the realities of daily life and the clamorous problems of the world. We must at least recover our expectancy that the spirit of Christ can renew the face of the earth, and the Kingdom be established among men. According to our faith it will be to us.

The central act of Christian worship is really charged with this confident expectation. Our Lord seems definitely to have declared that by His death a new age would have dawned. The world could never be the same again. 'From henceforth there shall be the Son of Man seated on the right hand of Power.' 'I will drink no more of this fruit of the vine until I drink it new in the Kingdom of God.' That conviction that His sacrifice was inaugurating a New Order, is inseparable from the Last Supper. We show forth the Lord's death *till He come*. One branch of the Church preserves this expectant outlook in its Eucharistic symbolism. In the Coptic churches the bread is freshly baked and taken still hot from the oven for consecration. 'Ye shall eat it in haste': there is no time to let it cool, as though life were normal and ordinary and slow. Unless you are quick, the Lord may have returned! The life communicated through the sacred elements is eternal life—'the life of the world to come'—offered us here and now in the fields of time, to turn Wapping into the City of God.

To learn to expect again that God will do things, to look for new irruptions of the Spirit coming in power like a rushing mighty wind, to rediscover God's availability—this is the hungry need of the Church to-day and the only hope of a disappointed world.

That is really the 'text' of all that follows. This book will attempt an elementary study of the expression of the Christian life in the complex civilization of to-day. It is not designed as a book on 'Christian Ethics', and I doubt if such a book can ever be written. For you cannot reduce Christianity to rule, or formulate it as a defined system. Christianity is a spirit, a life, an attitude, which must ever be clothing itself in new forms, which will break and re-form with the changing needs of history and the progressive experience of men. We approach it here as a dynamic principle informing and directing civilization rather than as a code of moral conduct. We shall base our study on a careful reading of the Epistle to the Ephesians, which is at once the most 'modern', in many ways, of all the books of the New Testament and the richest record of Christian experience. I do not propose to write a 'commentary' following the Epistle verse by verse. The day of such commentaries, perhaps, is past.[1] What we need now are broad interpretations of the answers which the books of the Bible offer to the challenge of our modern world. This book is offered as an Introduction to one of the most important of them all. We shall try, then, looking out upon our world—its facts, its problems, and its current thought—to apprehend St. Paul's contribution to the task which confronts our generation. This task it is no overstatement to call the reconstruction of civilization.

We can state the problem in its simplest terms. The problem of civilization is just this : how men and women are to live together in the best and richest possible human life. Thus civilization means co-operation. All the text-books show how man has passed through the family to the clan, through clan to tribe, through tribal fusions into the state proper. The straight line of historical development runs, plainly enough, still farther in this direction. Its goal is the union of the states themselves in a polity which shall embrace them all. But this is no 'automatic' evolution, and at present it is disastrously impeded. The development has been arrested, and the tendency to-day is retrogressive. 'The culmination of modern history'[2] in a world-wide international polity seems farther off than a century ago. Moreover, within the national groups themselves there are ominous signs of disintegration. The clash of interest in Industry seems almost to have reached breaking-point. 'Collective bargaining,' so hardly

[1] The 'final' commentary on *Ephesians* has been written by Dr. Armitage Robinson (Macmillan), and the 'Exposition' published separately at a low price. This is indispensable to the student.

[2] The reference is to Prof. Ramsay Muir's *Nationalism and Internationalism.*

won by the struggle and sacrifice of fifty years, protects the individual wage-earner from the relentless play of competitive 'selection'. But the Christian conscience cannot rest contented with a solution that frankly acquiesces in the idea of conflicting interests between the two partners in industrial enterprise. Indeed, the organization of Industry and that—on a wider stage—of the life of Nations, is directed permanently by fear; and we cannot regard these vast associations of massed economic and political terror as any equivalent of Christian 'fellowship' or of the real aim of civilized life. Between two groups which fear one another there cannot be effective co-operation. And the life of individuals within the groups is immeasurably stunted and impoverished by the sealing of their psychological frontiers.

Thus civilization to-day has reached an impasse. Organized, mutually exclusive groups—social, political, and economic—confront one another in undisguised hostility. There are all the elements here of a world-disaster. If human life is to endure at all, in any sense in which it is worth living, these groups have somehow got to be transcended and to take their place in a larger unity. A new Fellowship must be achieved, built on something more imperishable than the ties of mere self-interest and fear which hold the existing group-loyalties together. That must be done, or Western civilization must reel into inevitable dissolution.

That is our problem. And in times like these it is tempting enough to look back wistfully on the best aspects of the Middle Ages, when Europe was a spiritual unity in which, with whatever temporary antagonisms, men knew themselves fundamentally at one. Stoicism and the Roman Empire had prepared the way for the world-wide recognition of a unity behind all differences—of a moral and spiritual allegiance taking precedence of all local loyalties and binding the human race into one family. 'Dear City of God', said Marcus Aurelius, putting in his own severe language what St. Paul meant by 'Jerusalem above'. Already in the time of Hadrian the 'Law of the Nations' of the Roman law-courts had been identified with the Law of Nature common to all men (as the Stoics held) in virtue of their common reason.[1] The idea of this common spiritual unity, prior to and deeper than state-law, taken over and deepened by the Church, was the formative factor of the Middle Ages. It found its expression in the most magnificent of all the creations of human aspiration—the Papacy and the Holy Roman Empire. Men were not occupied then with our problems. Civilization *was* one: whatever differences there were—violent and frightful though they may have been—were differences within an existing unity. 'To be a Roman was to be a Christian, and the idea soon passed into the converse. To be a Christian was to be a Roman.'[2]

The problem for that world was less to achieve unity, than to save it from disruption. The Papacy was gloriously right in its tenacious unwillingness to countenance the break-up of that unity, and to give recognition to 'national' Christianity. The idea of merely National Churches was inconceivable to the mediaeval mind, and it is still wholly indefensible. A church which is only national is a contradiction in terms. But the forces at work were too strong to be resisted. When at the Council of Constance in 1414 the votes were recorded by *nations*, not by individuals, the beginning of the end was in sight. And, as we can see after the event, the Papacy was as definitely wrong in the attempt to impose a uniformity which ignored national and other differences on a world increasingly rich in variations. Nationalism was inevitable. The moral and spiritual drive behind it was the insurgent need for self-expression in free political activities without which human life loses half its meaning. To resist that was to resist the Spirit. Men must be the architects of their own social destinies; they must embody their hopes and aspirations in structures marked by their own particular temperament. And these will necessarily vary as much as human nature itself varies. The deep-seated weakness of the Roman Empire was that it had

[1] Bryce, *Studies in History and Jurisprudence*, ii. 142.

[2] Bryce, *Holy Roman Empire*, p. 13. Gregory of Tours said: 'Romanos vocitant homines nostrae religionis.'

eradicated variety. The whole pressure of the system was against any genuine individuality. The Empire eliminated personality. The imperial government, like the art of the period, was creating a depersonalized type, as a good bureaucracy always tends to do. It destroyed local political activity, and killed what might have become nationality. Caracalla's law denationalized the world. So the unity which the Christian Church inherited was a sign, in some ways, of death rather than life. And when Europe roused itself from its sleep again, it was inevitable that its renascent life should cut out the path that led to nation-hood. The mediaeval world was confronted with forces too strong and too complex for it to handle.

What was needed was such a unity as cannot be won by demanding uniformity. The mistake of the Papacy was the same mistake as is often made by Communism—the attempt to secure an effective unity by suppressing all subordinate ties and loyalties, lest they should come into collision with it. Plato, and many modern thinkers after him, have proposed to abolish the family, as competing for men's allegiance with the State. Others aim at subverting national patriotism in the hope that men may become 'Good Europeans'. The Roman Church was attempting the same short cut when it tried by overriding local loyalties to hold a common spiritual Empire. But not so is human nature constituted. It is only in and through the smaller loyalties that we come to understand the larger claim. The family is the school of citizenship. 'The State without the family is empty : the family without the State is blind'—so we might parody a famous sentence. So cosmopolitanism can never lead men into a unity higher than that of the Nation. What was needed then, and what we must recover now, is an arch-loyalty for the various groups, which shall not ignore their individualities, but give the fullest scope and expression to them, achieving its unity in their variety, while they come to themselves in that fuller co-operation. That is the only unity worth having. Had the Papal Court been able to understand this between the fourteenth and the sixteenth centuries, the whole tragedy might have been avoided, and the Great War might never have been fought. There is a lesson written in blood for us.

Thus uniformity is not unity. Indeed, if we think it out, there is no unity which does not comprise variety within it. The more variety, the more true the unity. Unless two things are really different they are not two things but one, and you cannot unify them. And, on the other hand, things are only 'unified' by taking their place in, and sharing, a common purpose. Thus the various notes which together form a melody are unified by the melody they express. And the unity of plan which is the melody is made possible only by their variety. You can make no tune by repeating a single note. The same is true of the lines and colours combined in the composition of a picture. And in human life the point is obvious. When modern psychology speaks about a 'crowd' (or 'group'), it does not mean any chance collection of people. It means a collection of people, great or small, who have something in common which unites them. A 'Football Crowd' is a group in this sense, by virtue of the common interest taken by all its members in the Cup-tie. It is this common interest which unifies them. And, from the psychological point of view, a club, a trade-union, or a Church are each a unity in this same sense. A single interest or purpose makes this collection of widely different people capable of thinking and acting together, and they in their infinite variety express the single purpose which unites them. The richer the variety of people and the more harmonious their co-operation, the nearer the group approaches perfect unity.

There was, as we have seen, a moment when the civilization of Western Europe had such a unity almost within its reach. It failed. And we, groping among the ruins which are the catastrophic price of that failure, have to make a fresh attempt to achieve it now. All serious thinkers and all men of goodwill are concerned with this central problem above all others. The appearance of Mr. Wells's *Outline of History*, however much expert scholars may criticize it, marks an epoch in the progress of popular thought. It interprets the unspoken intuitions which direct the hope of the people all over the world. 'How is Mankind to be organized into one community of knowledge and will?' Our task in this book is to make some sort of study of the specific contribution which Christianity offers to the problem.

The Church as an organized society is face to face with precisely the same problem as the secular civilization which surrounds her. The attempt to achieve a Reunion of the Church by the submission of the various bodies to absorption in a single uniformity is not merely impracticable: it implies a radically false ideal. Catholicity and Uniformity must not be regarded as interchangeable terms. A genuine unity of spirit demands variety of form. Certainly, we cannot rest contented with anything short of 'organic' unity—one Body as the instrument of the one Spirit of the whole. But this is consistent with—and indeed requires—the widest latitude within it for the varied manifestations and expressions of the Spirit which all share in common, adapted to the varying requirements of race, geography, and temperament. The Church's life can be a real unity only so far as each of the Christian bodies brings in its own distinctive contribution to the enrichment of the whole. And each distinctive body can find its fullness only by rising out of its limitations into the larger Christian loyalty. This is the wider Catholicity which inspired the Encyclical of Lambeth. Not by agreeing to 'sink our differences' in a vague lowest common denominator, nor by spreading a uniform-patterned paper over a wall that is gaping with rents and cracks, can effective Christian unity be won. 'It is only through a rich diversity of life and devotion that the unity of the whole Fellowship will be fulfilled.' [1]

Thus, both for the world and the Church which exists to save it, the controlling vision and need is that of Fellowship, in which the various conflicting groups can, without ceasing to be the groups they are, take their place in a wider unity. Such unity, finding its expression through all the different levels on which the loyalties of men constrain them, will give new wealth of meaning to them all

[1] *Report of Lambeth Conference (1920)*, p. 28.

and draw them into effective co-operation. This vision is floating before men's eyes to-day. All the best thought of the world is at work upon it—the elimination of international war, the harmonizing of 'class-interests', the organization of the world-state, the reunion of the Universal Church. 'God wills Fellowship' we say: and the tendency of the post-war generation is to interpret Christianity and the Kingdom of God in terms of the Coming Brotherhood.

The ideal has always haunted Western Europe. In the break-up and collapse of the old Empire which men had come to assume to be eternal, St. Augustine gave it a new definition in his great book on the City of God. All that was best and most characteristic in the spiritual unity of which the mediaeval world was conscious was controlled by the work of this great thinker. 'It is not too much to say', wrote Lord Bryce, 'that the Holy Roman Empire was built on the foundation of the *De Civitate Dei*.'[1]

In the quarrels between the Empire and the Papacy, both parties in the struggle appealed to this book as their authority, and it is possible to trace its influence all the way through the course of subsequent history.[2]

Moreover, after the crash came, the ideal was never wholly given up. After the triumph of 'pure politics' at the time of the Renaissance had opened up the age of Nationalism and the modern conception of the Balance of Power, there was still a consciousness of some higher unity constantly struggling to find expression. It is significant that the seventeenth century, the age of most unfettered nationalism, saw a revival and re-adaptation of the old Stoic and Christian Law of Nature in Grotius's writings on International Law.

We have seen the story repeated in our own day. The European war, though it intensified all the influences making for disunion, has also immeasurably deepened the longing for a new and higher unity. Within each of the combatant national groups under the pressure of the

[1] *Holy Roman Empire*, p. 93 note.

[2] This has been done with extraordinary skill in the late Dr. Figgis's *Political Aspects of St. Augustine's 'City of God'*.

common danger men became conscious of a new comradeship. Smaller loyalties were merged and each national group came to full self-consciousness. But there was nothing here that could endure. We had here simply a series of groups organized against one another, and with the removal of the immediate peril the sense of unity was bound to weaken. Thus, the disillusionment of so many to-day about the loss of the 'brotherhood of the trenches', however tragic it may be, was really from the first inevitable. A unity called into being by fear or hostility is no unity that can or should endure. Mr. Wilfrid Trotter has written well on this point. The common social instinct, he points out, has developed in different kinds of reaction. There is what he calls 'aggressive gregariousness', that which is manifested by the wolf-pack. There is the 'protective gregariousness' of weak things, exemplified familiarly in the sheep. And there is the more complex social structure of which the bee-hive is the animal type, united not for attack or defence alone but 'for all the activities of life'. This, which he calls 'socialized gregariousness', is—he says—'the goal of man's development'.[1] The fellowship of the trenches was far closer to the first and second type than to the third.

Further, the direct result of the late war has been the revival on a menacing scale of academic nationalist sentiments which men have now learnt to assert by force. 'Nationalism', as Lord Robert Cecil said, 'is the enemy'; and the Concert of Nations seems less attainable after 'the War to end war' than before. On the other hand, the very recognition of the devastating consequences of acquiescence in sheer nationalism has quickened the whole world to recognize the imperious need for transcending it. As in the seventeenth century, so now, out of the welter of national hostilities has grown a new longing for a League of Nations. This also, it is interesting to note, can be traced back to St. Augustine. His famous criticism of Imperialism contains a very striking passage in defence of what we now call 'small nationalities', which ends by suggesting that the peace of the world would

[1] *Instincts of the Herd in Peace and War*, p. 166.

best be secured by a number of small nations 'living gladly together in neighbourly agreement, as many small nations in the world as there are families in any State'.[1]

The desire is deeper, more seriously conceived, than ever it has been in previous history. The trouble is that our efforts are still paralysed by the popular despair of ever achieving it. What the world needs is a re-exploration of the resources of the Spirit of God, in drawing mankind into effective fellowship. 'It means an adventure of goodwill and still more of faith, for nothing less is required than a new discovery of the creative resources of God. To this adventure we are convinced that God is now calling His Church.' So wrote the Bishops in the Lambeth Appeal; and it is just this which St. Paul offers us in the book which we are now to study.

The topic of the Epistle to the Ephesians is of preeminent interest in the present day. 'At no former period has there been so widespread a recognition in all departments of human life of the need of combination and cooperation: and never, perhaps, has more anxious thought been expended on the problem of the destiny of mankind. . . . It is not too much to say that we who have begun to feel after the truth of a corporate life as higher than an individual life, are more eager than any past generation has been to learn, and perhaps are more capable of learning, what is the goal for which Man as a whole is making, or, in other words, what is God's Purpose for the Human Race.' So wrote the Dean of Wells in 1903. It is even more true in 1922. So much has happened since, such annihilating experiences and bitter lessons have come to the civilized world in the packed epoch of the last eight years, that in a sense we ask the question now with such new energy and in such perplexity as to make it almost

[1] 'Videant ergo ne forte non pertineat ad viros bonos gaudere de regni latitudine. Iniquitas enim eorum cum quibus iusta bella gesta sunt regnum adiuvit ut cresceret; quod ubique parvum esset si quies et iustitia finitimorum contra se bellum geri nulla provocaret iniuria; ac felicioribus sic rebus humanis omnia regna parva essent concordi vicinitate laetantia; et ita essent in mundo regna plurima gentium ut sunt in urbe domus plurimae civium.'—*De Civitate Dei*, iv. 15.

a new problem. That is our excuse for attempting here to travel afresh over the territory which Dean Armitage Robinson has made peculiarly his own. Intellectually and morally the background of post-war religious needs has taken on a vastly changed colour. The last generation recovered the conception of the organic life of the Catholic Church as the organ of the world's regeneration. To-day is its crisis and its opportunity. Christianity can have no meaning for the post-war generation unless it can show itself effective as the controlling spirit of a world-state and the basis of an enduring civilization. It must be the soul of the new League of Nations.

It was precisely thus that St. Paul conceived it. For him, as we shall see, the Christian Church is the real League of Nations.

The secret of its success is just this: that it recognizes that human fellowship can never be secured in two dimensions. It has to be rooted and grounded in the Eternal. Recent events have been a drastic commentary on the failure of two-dimensional civilization. Mankind can only live in this world successfully by recognizing that its true home is in another. So Paul strikes the keynote at the beginning by putting his scene 'in the heavenly places'.

For this cause I also, having heard of the faith in the Lord Jesus which is among you, and which *ye shew* toward all the saints, cease not to give thanks for you, making mention *of you* in my prayers; that the God of our Lord Jesus Christ, the Father of glory, may give unto you a spirit of wisdom and revelation in the knowledge of him; having the eyes of your heart enlightened, that ye may know what is the hope of his calling, what the riches of the glory of his inheritance in the saints, and what the exceeding greatness of his power to us-ward who believe, according to that working of the strength of his might which he wrought in Christ, when he raised him from the dead, and made him to sit at his right hand in the heavenly *places*, far above all rule, and authority, and power, and dominion, and every name that is named, not only in this world, but also in that which is to come: and he put all things in subjection under his feet, and gave him to be head over all things to the church, which is his body, the fulness of him that filleth all in all.—Eph. i. 15–23.

Wherefore, putting away falsehood, speak ye truth each one with his neighbour: for we are members one of another. Be ye angry, and sin not: let not the sun go down upon your wrath: neither give place to the devil. Let him that stole steal no more: but rather let him labour, working with his hands the thing that is good, that he may have whereof to give to him that hath need. Let no corrupt speech proceed out of your mouth, but such as is good for edifying as the need may be, that it may give grace to them that hear. And grieve not the Holy Spirit of God, in whom ye were sealed unto the day of redemption. Let all bitterness, and wrath, and anger, and clamour, and railing, be put away from you, with all malice: and be ye kind one to another, tenderhearted, forgiving each other, even as God also in Christ forgave you.—Eph. iv. 25–32.

CHAPTER II

THE BODY OF CHRIST

'The church, which is his body.'—Eph. i. 23.

'My Kingdom,' the Master had said, 'is not of this world.' Yet He taught men to pray, 'Thy Kingdom come on earth'. And these two phrases of His, taken together, are the best possible epitome of the Christian attitude to politics. The problems of human statesmanship, we hold, find their solution in another order—an eternal world which is not of time or space: but it has to be lived out in this world. Our real citizenship is in heaven: and *therefore* we are to be the better citizens of the actual cities where we dwell. In this way all true Christian idealism is firmly anchored to the world of facts. It is never merely 'lost in an O altitudo', nor is it ever the 'flight' of mystic pessimism. And therefore it succeeds where Plato failed.

The hope of men—as Plato saw so splendidly in an age that was ruled by no great principles—lies in the ordering of our politics by the light of the imperishable certainties. We, too, would have philosophers as Kings. We, too, would have all the activities of life correlated and controlled by the Vision of the Good. But the Philosopher of the *Republic,* in a world so full of blindness and violence, can do nothing but bow his head before the storm, waiting till the tyranny be overpast. And this is the very bankruptcy of idealism—the philosophy of Humpty Dumpty.

Nietzsche was quite right in charging Plato with importing 'other-worldliness' of the wrong sort into European thought. But the Christian insists that the philosopher must claim his Kingdom and be really King. The robuster faith of Christianity, because it knows that the city *is* 'above', works and prays to bring it down upon earth. The eternal order and the temporal cannot be conceived (we hold) as though they were in two parallel planes. The one is present in the other. The life of spirit which is simultaneous and—in communion with God—eternal, must live itself out in change and succession, its freedom only becoming operative in and through the 'necessity' of matter. In this way only can it be effective. This paradox runs through the whole of human life, giving it both its grandeur and its tragedy. Man—bounded in a nutshell and yet the king of infinite space, his mind in invention like a God, his body laid low by a draught or a mosquito sting—the whole greatness of his life is to be found in this very tension between the spiritual and the material, the conditioned and the free. He is, indeed, one of the least of creatures against the background of the Universe.

> When I consider the heavens, the works of thy fingers,
> The moon and the stars which Thou hast ordained,
> Then I say, 'What is man that Thou regardest him
> Or the son of man that Thou visitest him?'

Yet there is that in him which outsoars the stars and claims dominion over nature, by right of a higher and more abiding Order.

> Thou hast made him but little lower than God
> And crowned him with glory and honour:
> Thou hast given him dominion over the works of thy hands
> And put all things in subjection under his feet.

Born for communion with the Eternal—'to glorify God and enjoy Him for ever'—it is upon 'this earth our habitation' with all its transience and recalcitrancy that his life in God has to be expressed. Here is the central fact of Christianity. It is not only that the finite spirit has to live, as it were, in two worlds at once. The 'Father of Spirits' has Himself accepted this necessity of our existence. The Eternal has entered into the fields of time and lived the limited life of man among men. So we believe: and this faith carries with it, as its inescapable conclusion, the redemption of our entire existence here under the limitations of space and time, by the presence of the Eternal in it.

It was for this, as St. Paul holds, that the Church of Christ came into being—for the redemption of society, the perfecting of man's life in God. 'Christ loved the Church and gave Himself for her that He might present the Church to Himself in her glory, without flaw or blemish or any such thing, but that she might be holy and without reproach' (Eph. v. 3–27). And in this he truly interprets the mind of Christ. In what sense, if any, we can rightly hold that Jesus Himself discussed or contemplated the organization of the Church is too vast a question for a passing paragraph. We must be content here to leave it on one side. But whatever conclusion may be reached on that point, it is, I hold, quite firmly indisputable that the Church was called into being by His Spirit—that it is, in the strictest sense, 'His new creation'. It is true that the Christian Church was really founded on the day when the Master called the twelve about Him, and sent them forth to heal and to proclaim the Kingdom. Further, I think it is true that He did look forward to a society, in some form or other, to exhibit His way of life and proclaim His teaching. It is presupposed in the Sermon on the Mount. For new social relationships are there taken for granted. And it is implicit—making all allowances for the known ecclesiastical tendency in the record, for example, of St. Matthew—in not a few of the parables of the Kingdom. Von Hügel is fully justified in stressing this. It is very noticeable how frankly Our Lord accepts, and often seems to emphasize, the idea of social subordination, in the organic and articulate arrangement of man's social life, when illustrating His teaching about the Kingdom. Master and slave, employer and employed, sovereign and subject, Government and taxpayer, buyer and seller, father and family—all these find their place in the best-known parables. We are right to give full value to facts like these.

But in any case, even if it should be held that this line of argument fails to bring conviction, there remains one unchallengeable assertion. What Jesus actually said is one thing: what His teaching really implied may be another. And it is impossible to question that a new and all-including social life, cutting across all barriers and divisions, is a *necessary* implication of His teaching about the Divine Fatherhood. Nor can it be seriously disputed that Our Lord believed that in some sense or other the new Society, organized by the new revelation of God, would be brought into existence by His death. 'I, if I be lifted up from the earth, will draw all men unto me.' Already, even in the Synoptic Gospels, in the record of His final teaching, the word 'Covenant' takes its place side by side with the more familiar 'Kingdom'.[1]

This was the world-wide Church that Jesus died for: and this is the real and only League of Nations. And St. Paul beyond doubt had caught the Master's outlook —had, as he claimed himself, the Mind of Christ—when he helped it so splendidly to achievement. His insistence that there is now neither Jew nor Gentile, Man nor Woman, Slave nor Free—that is, that the deepest and most enduring cleavages in the social structure of the world he knew had been annulled by the new revelation—is in the true spirit of the High-priestly prayer (St. John xvii). Here again, of course, we are faced by a critical problem. But it is probable that every one who has genuinely thought about Our Lord's teaching will agree that whether or not that great chapter reports words actually used by Jesus, it is a superbly true interpretation of thoughts that were deep and central in His mind. And a highly significant fact here comes to light under the analysis of criticism. Put the New Testament in its historical order, and it is clear that so soon as Christianity came to be understood in terms of the Spirit then, from that moment, UT OMNES UNUM SINT ('that they all may be one') was recognized to be its truest expression.

The Church was certain that 'God wills Fellowship'. Looking out across the contemporary world it saw 'great gulfs' dividing man from man. But it also saw that *God did not fix them.* It was as in the parable of the

[1] Mark xiv. 25, and parallels.

Master: men had acquiesced in dividing gulfs, and they had become irrevocable destinies which needed a miracle of Grace to bridge them. But the great miracle was being performed. All were becoming 'one man in Christ Jesus'. That was the primary aim of the Church's life. In their growing experience of the Lord, as well as from the records of His teaching, they had learnt from Him that 'God wills Fellowship'. And when the Church offered her daily prayer, 'Our Father, thy will be done on earth,' that, if she truly prayed in the name of Christ, was the first and primary thing she meant. God wills a new social integration: the Church is in the world to achieve it.

Thus we must hold that the Church which produced the New Testament is a true development of Galilee. The historical vindication of this faith in the unification of mankind, as well as the strongest force that went to the making of it, was the decisive experience of Pentecost. St. Luke's account tends to obscure the more permanent elements in this event, and throws into relief what was temporary and local—the phenomena of ecstasy and 'tongue-speaking'. But it was the turning-point of civilization. It was, for the first time in human history, the emergence of the ideal social life into the plane of time and space. Here for the first time was a community in which the humblest individual member, fulfilling his allotted function, found his full self-expression in the service of the whole, while the common purpose of the whole verified itself completely in the life of each of its individual members. There was differentiation without division: there was an intense unity subsisting in a full and rich variety. The members were many—of many different sorts—and yet they were, as St. Paul put it, one (ἕν) in a single satisfying purpose which gave meaning and coherence at once to the group and to its component members. 'The multitude of the believers were of one heart and of one soul.' And further, the inward spiritual unity which organized the new society was expressed outwardly in its economic life. 'There was not any among them that lacked: none thought that his possessions were his own.'[1] They belonged, as the Master had said, to Another (St. Luke xvi. 12) Who was the directing will of the community. Thus private property was made compatible with the fullest recognition of social duty. Wealth has never been so completely 'socialized' as it was in the Church of the first four centuries.[2]

This society was the first creation of the spirit of the Risen Christ. Jesus clothed Himself in this Church. Henceforth the idea of the Community (κοινωνία) is inseparable from the thought of the Spirit. As the Christian consciousness developed, Christ-Spirit and Christ-Body were seen with increasing clearness to be inseparable. To be a partaker of the Spirit and to communicate in and with the Body were conceived and spoken of as much the same thing. This experience of Pentecost was paramount. It controlled all subsequent developments. More and more as the cruder interpretations of the gifts of the Spirit came to be discarded—mainly, it seems, under St. Paul's influence—its lasting significance was understood in terms of the ethical life of the society. It meant living together in love and joy and peace, rather than speaking unintelligibly.

New and great adventures had to be dared before the Church could come to full self-knowledge. Most tremendous and most searching was the undreamt-of lifting of her horizon so that it might include the Gentile world. This was the signal achievement of St. Paul as the inheritor of St. Stephen's faith, though with the full concurrence of St. Peter. But though St. Paul helped the Church to realize, more clearly than before his conversion, what her own faith and life really involved, he demonstrated by the logic of facts something which had been all the time implied in it. It was the society that was born at Pentecost which determined the course of St. Paul's own development. In his great description of the Body of Christ he is not imagining a new ideal so much as

[1] Acts iv. 32. I take this to mean that the primitive Church did not practise an actual communism, though many authorities think otherwise, and St. Luke, elsewhere, suggests that it did (Acts ii. 44, 45).

[2] For this paragraph see Anderson Scott in *The Spirit*, chap. iv.

appealing to an existing fact. He made the conception richer and more ample: he gave it lucidity and definition. But he may be said to be only etching in more sharply and more permanently lines that had been already plainly visible in the earliest Jerusalem community. He is writing with one eye on the Upper Room. He is working out the significance of Pentecost—that is, ultimately, of the Resurrection—for the social progress of mankind.

The world is coming to sit at his feet again. It would be almost everywhere agreed to-day that it was a disastrous declension from the outlook of the New Testament when the 'salvation' of the individual was made the dominant aim of the Christian mission. It was untrue to the facts of human nature as well as to the genius of Christianity. And in our own time we have seen a recovery—some may think even an exaggeration—of the social interpretation of our religion. To this two main forces have contributed. Inside the English Church the Oxford Movement, as the necessary reaction from the evangelical revival, realized that personal religion demands the social and institutional contacts for the building up of the religious life, as well as prophets and evangelists to force the initial challenge home.[1] On the wider terrain, the leading tendency of the various branches of modern sociology—Anthropology, Comparative Religion, and most strongly of all, perhaps, Social Psychology—has been to emphasize very heavily the essentially social nature of Religion. We shall see below (Chapter VI) that, as was to be expected, this reaction tends to overreach itself. But it is clear gain that we can now assume that Christianity is to be understood as the principle of an organized social life.

The late Prof. Royce's Gifford Lectures typified the rediscovery of the social expression of the Christian faith. He finds the essence of Christianity to consist in loyalty to the Beloved Community,[2] losing our-

[1] Cf. the significant praise of the Roman Catholic missions from this standpoint in Schweitzer's *On the Edge of the Primaeval Forest*, p. 166.

[2] Cf. Swinburne's 'Love, the beloved Republic, which feeds upon freedom and lives' (*Hertha*).

selves in its service and identifying ourselves with its welfare. In this he is very close to St. Paul's thought. But there is, all the same, a divergence which reaches down to absolute fundamentals. It is that, as Canon Quick wrote several years ago,[1] the Beloved Community of Prof. Royce is offered to our reverence—decapitated. Royce tended to leave out the Head of the Body. In this the book may fairly be regarded as typical of a wide-spread modern tendency. People tend to discuss the Christian Institutions from a purely sociological standpoint, omitting that unique factor in them which makes them specifically what they are—the Personality of Christ. This is something absolutely vital. There is involved here the entire difference between the answer given by Christianity to the main problem of our civilization and that which is given by Social Psychology. We shall be concerned with this in later chapters. We shall find ourselves led to maintain that St. Paul's conception is at once more scientifically adequate and more workable in practice than that of a non-supernatural Sociology. It must be sufficient here to note the difference.

Meantime, it needs no argument to show that the Personality of Jesus is absolutely central in St. Paul's thought. 'Christ in you' is for him 'the hope of Glory'. And here, while definitely 'Catholic'[2] in the main stresses of his teaching, he may be held to correct that dangerous tendency to what is commonly called ecclesiasticism, which is latent in the 'Catholic' position. It is doubtless true that St. Paul would find no meaning in the idea of an individual Christian not thought of in relation to the Church. But neither would he attach any value to the thought of the Church as an end in its own right. It was, for him, the direct and immediate effect of the operation of the Christ-Spirit. It had value and meaning only as 'unto' Him. St. Paul's whole theory and practice are

[1] *Modern Philosophy and the Incarnation*, p. 41.

[2] I use 'Catholic' here in the restricted sense in which it is now current, as the modern equivalent of Newman's 'High Church'. I think this is an abuse of the word; but as it is now so commonly used in this sense I adopt it here, with inverted commas, to save a periphrasis.

unintelligible except in terms of the personal, risen Jesus, who is Himself the Head of the Body, and is making it the expression of His will. How else could he have justified his rulings on points of ecclesiastical discipline by the staggering assertion 'We have the mind of Christ'? This shows sufficiently what he himself thought about it. It remains still to ask whether what he thought was true.

It may or may not be the case—we have left it open—that our Lord Himself before the Crucifixion thought or spoke about what became 'the Church' as an ecclesiastical institution. But we have claimed that what happened after Pentecost was at once the creation of His spirit and the necessary development of the Galilean preaching. We can say this, of course, and still be free to recognize that at this or that point historical Christianity may have missed or misinterpreted His mind. I believe it to be quite certain that it has done so. But the 'advanced' theory that St. Paul was the real inventor of Christianity—turning the teaching of the synagogue and hill-side into a sacramental mystery-cult, and distorting the whole purpose of the Master—seems to me utterly untenable in the face of any critical inquiry.

All the evidence tends to contradict it. Whether we like it or not, the Church was 'Catholic' almost as soon as it became a Church—possibly before St. Paul joined it. It was the Church that taught Paul his 'Catholicism'. We cannot here discuss this even cursorily. But, on the point which immediately concerns us, we may note how constantly St. Paul is quite obviously basing his utterances on reminiscences of the words of Jesus. When he is most solemnly protesting against misrepresentation of the Gospel, his appeal is not to the Christ of the Church's experience, but to the historic Jesus. 'Another Jesus whom we have not proclaimed,' is his verdict on the rival teacher's doctrine (2 Cor. xi. 4).

Notice, too, that he definitely equates his own experience outside Damascus with that of the other Resurrection-Visions granted to those who had known Christ in the flesh. That St. Paul knew Christ in spiritual experience and not in the days before the Crucifixion is obvious enough from his own statements. But such knowledge can well be more intimate rather than less. And I think it grows clear, on a sympathetic reading of the correspondence of St. Paul by any one who knows the synoptic Gospels, that the Spirit-Christ of the Pauline cultus is indeed the Jesus of history. Let us remember that the Synoptic Gospels were written as a deliberate attempt to get back behind the experience of the apostolic age, and recall 'what it felt like' before the Resurrection to stand and listen to Him in the crowd. The Pauline Churches had been there for years—some fifteen years before the Marcan Document, and correspondingly longer before the others—and the synoptic Gospels were accepted by those Churches (who had never seen Him) as a true portrait of the Christ they knew. This is a most impressive piece of evidence.

More than this, it is clear enough to us that there were points at which St. Paul's teaching was immeasurably *more* true to the mind of Christ than was that of some who had known the historic Jesus. This certainly holds of the Universalism which he got accepted by a reluctant Church—the doctrinal sanction of the Gentile mission. It is also true of the way he interpreted the attitude of Christ to the Jewish law. St. James and others would have claimed for it an eternal place in the Christian community. St. Paul said that it was the Paidagogos who takes the boy to school *and then goes away* while the teacher does his work (Gal. iii. 24). Its work was done: it had brought men to Christ's school. On both these points he was a suspected modernist: but on each it was he who best knew the Master's mind.

Thus, to sum up, we may make bold to assert that it was no other than the historic Jesus who was the centre of St. Paul's life and thought, and the Head of his ideal world-community. It was, indeed, with St. Paul as with St. Peter at the crucial moment at Caesarea Philippi. It was upon his venturesome allegiance to the person of his Greatest Friend—on *this* rock that the Master built His Church, and the Gates of Hell have not prevailed against it.

It was clear that the Spirit of the historic Jesus, as the Spirit of perfected human life in perfect union with the life of God, could only express itself in a society, and must realize itself in time and space. Spirit must always make itself a body as the instrument for its self-expression. And St Paul saw that the new Society, cutting across all lesser relationships, was the Body in which the Risen Christ had clothed Himself. It was the essential work and manifestation of the New Life in the world of men. The organized life of the New Society, in all its functions and relationships, was to be the revelation here on earth of the Spirit of the Risen Christ in Heaven. Through it He revealed Himself to the world, as the personality of Paul revealed itself through his speech and act and gesture. So that the perfecting of the Fellowship was, in a phrase that has now become conventionalized, the extension of the Incarnation. By this should all men know they were His disciples, by their love one to another. And that was, in fact, what actually happened. And this sacramental principle permeates the whole of St. Paul's thought. It found its highest expression in the Eucharist, in which 'communion in the Body of Christ', in the sense of incorporation in the Fellowship, was never clearly distinguished, even in thought, from personal communion with the LORD. 'Communion' and 'Fellowship' stand for the same Greek word (κοινωνία), of which 'Community' is the best translation. But the Church itself was the supreme sacrament. The life of the Church was to mediate the Christ-life and make it visible to men. That was, clearly, what the Church was for—to be doing what He had been doing in the flesh, showing forth the character of God and revealing 'love in a life'.

This Spirit came into a definite world. It had to accept and declare itself through definite historical conditions. As a seed clothes itself from its environment, so must the Spirit which organized the Church. It could not operate in a vacuum. It must use and make instrumental to itself whatever was malleable in the imperial world—the Greek mysteries, the Roman law, all that made the fabric of Christian institutionalism. But

what St. Paul never did. He seeks to 'present every man perfect in Christ': but he knows that no individual personality can adequately mirror the Christ-life. It is the *Society* which is His Body. For him, it needed the whole human race to be the revelation of Christ's spirit. His is the perfect Personality—the Fullness (πλήρωμα) is his word—which is all-including. Each individual disciple can reflect some ray or aspect of that character. But the bearer or subject of the Christ-Personality is the entire Church, 'which is His Body'. The Church, as her life widens and increases, is gradually 'growing up into Christ'. The goal of individual believers is to grow *not* into perfected individuals, but, through the unity of faith and knowledge, all together into Perfect Man—the completed expression of Personality, the measure of the stature of the fullness of Christ (Eph. iv. 13). We can only tell what is meant by Personality when the Christ has drawn the whole world about Himself and fulfilled Himself in the new world-Fellowship. Such is St. Paul's magnificent conception.

We may note incidentally that this idea implies that the question, 'What is Christianity?' is one which, strictly speaking, is still unanswerable. The Christ, as St. Paul audaciously declares, is still 'coming to His fulfilment'.[1] Until the Church of Christ has achieved her Mission and organized the whole race in her Fellowship we do not know 'what we shall be'. And this knowledge, perhaps, can never come on earth (Chapter VI below). Only we know that the highway of our progress is an increasingly adequate expression in the social integrations of mankind of the life which is in Jesus.

[1] Eph. i. 23: see Armitage Robinson's note.

CHAPTER III

CHRISTIANITY AND SOCIAL PSYCHOLOGY

And you *did he quicken*, when ye were dead through your trespasses and sins, wherein aforetime ye walked according to the course of this world, according to the prince of the power of the air, of the spirit that now worketh in the sons of disobedience; among whom we also all once lived in the lusts of our flesh, doing the desires of the flesh and of the mind, and were by nature children of wrath, even as the rest:—but God, being rich in mercy, for his great love wherewith he loved us, even when we were dead through our trespasses, quickened us together with Christ (by grace have ye been saved), and raised us up with him, and made us to sit with him in the heavenly *places*, in Christ Jesus: that in the ages to come he might shew the exceeding riches of his grace in kindness toward us in Christ Jesus: for by grace have ye been saved through faith; and that not of yourselves: *it is* the gift of God: not of works, that no man should glory. For we are his workmanship, created in Christ Jesus for good works, which God afore prepared that we should walk in them.—Eph. ii. 1–10.

Finally, be strong in the Lord, and in the strength of his might. Put on the whole armour of God, that ye may be able to stand against the wiles of the devil. For our wrestling is not against flesh and blood, but against the principalities, against the powers, against the world-rulers of this darkness, against the spiritual *hosts* of wickedness in the heavenly *places*. Wherefore take up the whole armour of God, that ye may be able to withstand in the evil day, and, having done all, to stand. Stand therefore, having girded your loins with truth, and having put on the breastplate of righteousness, and having shod your feet with the preparation of the gospel of peace; withal taking up the shield of faith, wherewith ye shall be able to quench all the fiery darts of the evil *one*. And take the helmet of salvation, and the sword of the Spirit, which is the word of God—Eph. vi. 10–18.

CHAPTER III

CHRISTIANITY AND SOCIAL PSYCHOLOGY

'That he might create in himself of the twain one new man, *so* making peace; and might reconcile them both in one body unto God through the cross, having slain the enmity thereby.'—Eph. ii. 15, 16.

THE tendencies of contemporary thought are moving swiftly back to the New Testament. Right outside theological thought and writing, in social psychology and kindred sciences, there is a swing back to St. Paul's position. For several centuries the hardest thinking about the structure of Society has moved among conceptions far too abstract. Theories of political obligation are a familiar study at the universities, and the very name explains what is really lacking. The jurists who applied the Stoic principles naturally approached political problems from a legal and contractual point of view. 'What is the legal basis of Sovereignty?' This was the question with which they were really occupied. The resulting discussion was strangely academic. It is true that most of them were chiefly anxious to find a theoretical vindication for their own political preferences. Thus Hobbes's *Leviathan* is an elaborate pamphlet against the theory of divine right, but strongly in favour of absolute Government. Locke and Rousseau, from widely different standpoints, are supporting the revolutionary movements, so different in form, in their respective countries. But, all the same, it is scarcely possible to read any of these famous writers without feeling that they are singularly unreal. They were treating politics like mathematics. They left unexplored the real heart of the problem—human nature and its constitution. They took little account of the human and moral facts which, after all, control jurisprudence. So they seem to us depressingly doctrinaire. Their work seems, like the scholastic theology, to be building up towering *a priori* systems but rarely handling the living tissues which go to form both politics and religion. It is, perhaps, not without significance that the books we have been discussing date from the centuries when the mathematical sciences were dominant.

There came, of course, the inevitable reaction. For one wild period in the nineteenth century men were intoxicated by the inrush of the new biological discoveries, and Biology reigned over the world of thought. This made a profound impression on social theory. Men pressed back behind abstract speculation to grapple afresh with the facts of the situation. There arose a new interest in social origins, and the 'blessed word' Evolution dominated thought about Society. To Prussia it came as a new Gospel, supplying a plausible scientific basis for the cruder lusts of national ambition. Here was a justification in high theory for the beast which wars within us against the god. Human life is a struggle for existence. 'Each for himself and the devil take the hindmost'—that is the fundamental law of the Universe. 'Competition is the law of life.' Such was the ethic which came to be accepted not only in Germany but all over Europe, imposingly buttressed, as it seemed, by Science. It is hardly to be denied that this common outlook helped to set in train the disastrous tendencies which came to their ruinous issue in the world-war. So great a price must men pay for false thinking.

For it was, indeed, an intellectual sophistry. It must be recognized as a great advance in man's control over his own destiny when the general principles of evolution came to be universally accepted. An attempt was made to come to terms with facts. The pre-human origins of human life were allowed full value in men's calculations. But the trouble was that they were allowed too much. People were occupied with the ape and tiger, forgetting that man is after all neither an ape nor a tiger but a man. The distinctively human facts were still left out. There can be no adequate theory of human nature which leaves out that which makes it what it is, namely, moral personality. It is true enough that within human life natural selection is still operative. It is not true that the 'survival of the fittest' is necessarily connected with human progress. Man is essentially a moral being, and no purely biological categories can be adequate to measure his social life.

There was here then, we shall admit, a real attempt to base politics on human nature. But it rested on half-truths about human nature. And the same sort of criticism fairly holds against the economic view of society. It, too, was an attempt to be true to facts; but because it only considered half the facts, it has been followed by disastrous consequences. Countless children were offered up in England as human sacrifices to the 'laws of Economics'.

Now here again it is obviously true that the economic factor looms very large in the ordering of society. To neglect it cannot fail to be ruinous. Thus the unhappy Austrian Republic created by the Treaty of Versailles was a state conceived as a purely political fact, set up in economic isolation, and therefore doomed to perish by starvation, as is actually happening to-day. And, again, the possibility of achieving a free and worth-while life for millions of Europeans at this moment depends very largely on stabilizing the Exchanges. There is no doubt that many a well-meaning Utopia would collapse like a house of cards at its first contact with the operation of economic law. Yet we have to remember what Christ once asserted—that any human structure will collapse unless its foundations are built beneath the surface, on the rock of spiritual and moral principle (Matt. vii. 24). It is exaggerating a truth till it becomes a destructive fallacy if we allow economic laws to be regarded as real laws of the Universe. Behind economics lie men : behind money, the wills of those who earn and spend it. Our generation knows the appalling difficulty of moulding the system of industry to our will and making it the instrument of spirit. The machine which men created to be their slave has become a tyrannical and savage master, crushing its creators between its wheels. But, however great the difficulty, it is our prerogative to claim the right. The laws of money are not like the law of gravity. For over and above economic law stands the higher law of the moral order, and the wills and desires of human personalities.

The so-called 'laws' of economics are the tabulated results of the observation of human 'behaviour' in this sphere of life. They are not inherent in the nature of things. If men become different, so will their behaviour: but the real laws of the Universe would not. No change of heart on the part of an astronomer is likely to affect the law of gravity: but it *would* affect the 'way his money goes'.

Thus, to write history or to direct policy from an exclusively economic standpoint does as much violence to the actual facts as a purely biological approach. What is needed is a point of view which will reckon fearlessly and squarely with the physical and material foundations on which man's life as a moral being rests, but will recognize that moral personality is the very differentia of man. It must be seen that while indisputably the more primitive elements in our constitution do supply the material for our moral life, they are at least equally penetrated by it and thereby given a different quality. 'How much better is a man than a sheep!'

And this is the strength of contemporary Psychology. The investigation of the racial instincts, the laws and processes at work in the evolution of Society, is a recognized department of social science. It is seen now that the problem of Society is neither wholly biological nor wholly a matter of material needs. It is in its essence psychological. That is to say it is psycho-physical. It involves the training and co-ordination of the instincts, sentiments, and desires of men. And this, after all, is what Christianity has said with monotonous reiteration ever since it has said anything. Dr. MacDougall is probably right in claiming that the new science of Social Psychology must revolutionize our social theories—also, no doubt, to some extent, our ethics. We are out of the region of doctrinaire abstraction and back again in contact with the facts: and also, we are close to the mind of St. Paul. He does not, of course, use (and we may be thankful for it) either the categories or the technical language of our modern social science. But he is concerned with precisely the same problem—the training of man's affections and desires, the education of his will, the sublimation of his instincts in the life of the Great Society. He brings us face to face with the facts again. He recognizes fully how intractable is the material with which we have to deal. He knows the strength of the anti-social impulses and how hard it is to train them socially. But he does not, like so many of our contemporaries, leave out the central fact of human life. He knows what God can do with human nature. The problem then was, as the problem in all ages will be, the socializing of mankind; and St. Paul declares that Jesus Christ has done it, by the appeal which he makes to men's allegiance, by the redirecting and transforming of their instincts and desires through the influence of His Spirit on them.

Christianity has never pretended that men and women have not bodies. Its faith is centred in an Incarnation, in which the physical basis of human life and the fundamental impulses and tendencies common to us and our animal ancestry were made the instrument of the eternal Spirit. There is a certain higher materialism which always keeps the best Christian thought sane and anchored to life's realities. But it is, on the other hand, a standing protest against what is now a most popular fallacy. Our generation is obsessed by preoccupation with man's origins. Christianity is more interested in his goal. No doubt it was salutary and greatly needed that what calls itself the 'New Psychology' should warn us against a bloodless 'spirituality' which ignores the constitution of human life. It was right that students and teachers of religion should be forcibly reminded that the higher spiritual life of men is built on the basis of animal impulses, and that we ignore them at our peril. In so far as we have tended to forget this we have drifted away from the central Christian teaching. For, after all, the whole religious importance of an Incarnation in the flesh is the redemption not of the human *soul* but of human life in all its range and depth, all its moral and psychological levels being penetrated by the supernatural and made the organ of eternal Life. That is inherent in the Christian doctrine. But that is by no means the same thing as to give precedence to what is primitive. At the present time there is still a queer tendency to think that what you can trace to an animal origin is of more importance than those higher processes, evolved by mankind in its long history, which differentiate man from the animals. In the same way there are many who seem to wish to give precedence over will and reason to those dark sub-conscious processes outside the focus of our conscious life. It is well to realize the extent to which these processes do enter into the stream of waking consciousness. It is well to know that by understanding them we can gain fresh mastery over circumstances and be more fully masters of ourselves. But to suggest that sub-rational processes are more important or of higher worth than the activities of conscious reason, is to part company with sane thinking. We can better understand the finished product, whether it be a thing or a human life, if we know something of its origins; but if we think of nothing but its origins we simply have not begun to understand it. To think of man chiefly in terms of animal life is to give up thinking about man at all. What matters, after all, about human life is not that it has emerged from bestial origins, but that it has ascended towards God. The important thing is not that men and women are distantly related to the anthropoids, but that God can make human nature the instrument of His own self-revelation, and that the basic instinct of gregariousness can be so trained as to express itself in spiritual Fellowship. St. Paul in this book, then, is keeping close to facts. He is studying the make-up of human nature, the heights and depths of which man's heart is capable. But he is not neglecting the main factor. He builds his philosophy upon human nature, when the Spirit of Christ has got to work upon it. Thus St. Paul's, like all the best Christian thought, takes the problem with which he is concerned—the problem of organizing human fellowship—with an infinitely greater seriousness than some modern thinkers who pride themselves on their realism.

As we look back over a hundred years, we can see what a desperate load of misery has been laid on our unhappy world by superficial views of human nature. The Utilitarian School of thought prided itself on its faithfulness to human fact. But it started from the false assumption that self-interest is the only motive of action—a view which certainly cannot face the light of better psychological knowledge. The 'economic man' is a mere abstraction. And it also supposed that, in some astounding way, if all men would pursue their own interests they would be serving the interest of the whole. Thus, by an ever-increasing selfishness and the play of uncontrolled competition, the Millennium was to be ushered in. That is, they tried by deliberately fostering the anti-social impulses of men to achieve a transcendent social good. This was accepted by men of first-rate intellect. It succeeded in inspiring Tennyson with an almost mystic exaltation. 'Locksley Hall' and the Great Exhibition were the outward symbols of this hope. The disillusionment came, as was inevitable. 'Locksley Hall' looked very different to the poet's imagination 'sixty years after'. God had given them their desire, and sent leanness withal into their souls. And the falling-in of the structure of Western Europe in August 1914 was the logical conclusion of this fallacy. It had been an attempt to build up civilization on a bridge thrown across the bottomless pit. The Cobdenite belief in Commerce as 'God's international law' has thus been drastically discredited. And the abandonment of this ideal—this prosperous and self-satisfied philosophy—is sheer gain to the Race. Against such a philosophy as this Christ comes not with peace but with a sword.

But human nature is deeper than men knew, and the problem far more complex than they realized. Christianity does take big issues seriously. It knows that the key to the problem of civilization lies very deep down in the heart of man, in his moral and spiritual constitution. It knows, too, that the life of man runs back into an unseen and eternal background, and that, if you leave that out of your calculations, you have not come near to the truth about human life. Just as psychologists insist to us that the explanation of our simplest actions lies deep down out of sight in the sub-conscious, so Christianity asserts that the clue to the practical problems of daily life, the organization of society and the proper ordering of industry, lies far back in the depths of another Order, where the roots of man's life strike down into God. It knows that the achievement of democracy is ultimately a spiritual problem. It has needed the cross of Christ to make it possible.

It is easy to put two rivals in one boat, but if they still row in opposite directions they will only succeed in breaking the boat in halves. It is easy to set two men side by side: the problem is how to teach them to enjoy it. And this is the whole problem of the world: how to make men *want* to pull together. It is, as we shall see, deeply imbedded in the thought of St. Paul and the whole New Testament that the crucifixion of Christ makes this possible. It is the Cross of Christ which has 'slain the enmity'. It is Christ conquering by His Cross who supplies the 'expulsive power of a new affection', drawing men from conflicting sectional instincts to desire and to live for a new common good.

Much has been written about the necessity of finding a moral equivalent of war. The trouble is that the knowledge of what is good does not secure that man will desire to do it. The knowledge of our community of interest is not enough to make us act in common. We may know, and men have known for many years, that in the complexity of modern life it is sober fact that if one member suffers all the other members suffer with it. We may know, as all the world knows now to its cost, that war brings no profit to conqueror or conquered. And yet we still do go to war. That is to say, there must be something more than recognition of the truth of demonstrable principles. There must be something with an appeal in it, to make men desire it and yield their wills to it; and this is precisely what Christianity offers. The great conception of the Kingdom of God in which Love shall be the only King, inaugurated by the Cross of Christ, is alone sufficiently great and appealing enough to secure the allegiance of the world, to draw to itself the desires and wills of men and to offer an outlet for our deepest instincts in a co-operative social life. And here we can claim Mr. Wells as among the prophets. The metaphysics of *God the Invisible King* were discouragingly superficial: they gave no answer whatever to their own question. But the great chapter on the Kingdom of God as the unfailing purpose of mankind, which shall be a central object of desire for all classes, nations, sects, and interests, each asking the other, 'What are you doing for It?', lies very near to the thought of the New Testament.

When all has been said, the fundamental weakness of the views which we have been criticizing is that they place man's life on too shallow a stage. They see it framed by the order of time and space, and have no idea of the depths that lie behind it. The assumption of all these theories is, at bottom, that a man's life does consist in the abundance of things which he possesses. The cardinal assertion of religion is that life conceived under such terms just is not truly life at all. Ever since the rise of 'real' politics, Europe at any rate has been attempting to base its life on a This-world foundation: the foundation has cracked and the superstructure fallen in. The late war was the criticism of history on a purely humanistic civilization: and the terrors of the Peace have underlined it. I do not complain of a financial basis for the organization of society merely because it is 'un-idealistic', but because it is practically unworkable. Examine the concrete issue of Reparations as it presented itself two years ago. Justice demanded reparation. The aggressor must be prepared to pay the price. And yet it was impossible to demand this without involving the other side in ruin. If the Central Powers should pay their debts in gold, then they would cease to be potential buyers, and the Allied Powers would be inevitably involved in the bankruptcy of their best market. If, on the other hand, they paid in goods, the Allies' factories must close down and the conquering nations endure unemployment as the price of exacting justice from the conquered. The facts give us here a bitter commentary on the practical failure in terms of common-sense of a civilization based on economics. For behind economic facts lie human wills: behind economic 'laws' is the moral order. So Christianity has always warned us, and the world is being forced at present by the relentless pressure of hard facts to consider again the Christian view of things and the eternal bases of civilization. 'Love not the world', for the world 'passeth away': only in the Eternal is security.

Let us examine how 'practical' St. Paul is. Christianity, which claims to be a faith and a life for man in Society, must come to terms with Social Psychology. 'A few statesmen sitting round a table can never hope to devise and put in motion a complete working system which will abolish war, abate national rivalries, and create a positive living world-organism. . . . The notion that a living effective world-federation can be manufactured to order is a good example of that unpractical idealism which imagines that a scheme of such magnitude can be realized at once because it is an admirable ideal scheme. . . . In this case what must be attained is a harmony between the organization of herd instinct in the national and partial herd-form with a new organization of universal herd instinct.' [1]

Something of this kind is what St. Paul would say if he were writing his letter to our modern world. It is precisely this with which he is occupied. *Ephesians* is a study of social psychology from the point of view of Christian experience. His concern (and, as we shall see, his achievement) is the organization of the Group-mind through all the hierarchy of subordinate groupings, in a group coterminous with Civilization. Our world is a different world from his: our horizons are wider, our life far

[1] Tansley, *New Psychology*, p. 216.

more complex. We do not think in terms of Jew and Gentile, but of Nationalism and Internationalism, Labour and Capital, white and coloured races. But his principles are every bit as valid and as patient of practical application in 1923 as they were in 60. Both his problem and his answer to it are singularly *en rapport* with the needs and the thought of the world in which we are living.

Psychology warns us—and we need the warning—that no scheme of social reconstruction can have any hope of success or fruitfulness if it ignores the fundamental instincts on which the associations of mankind rest. It must co-operate with nature, using not violating natural tendencies. And this is inherent in Christianity. God, for us, was made manifest in flesh, and therefore we seek to consecrate and spiritualize the order of nature, not to escape from it. So that we must keep close to the 'gregarious' instinct. But instinct—as psychology assures us—is a force which has to be trained and educated. Instinct by itself is 'not enough'. It will not bring us into a world-polity. Indeed, as we shall show in a later chapter, the *crude* operation of the gregarious instinct, if left to merely natural reactions and not evoked by a supernatural 'stimulus', rather hinders than advances social progress. But it is of the very nature of an instinct that though it is innate in our constitution and can therefore never be eradicated or safely left out of our calculations, yet it can be trained and educated—*sublimated,* as the text-books have it—along ever higher channels of response. And so it must be with the instinct of the herd. It will be the instrument of full social life in the rich sense which is called by Christians 'love' only when it is called into action not by mere 'group sentiment', but in conscious answer to the love of God.

Thus it is that the racial inheritance which goes to the making of our human nature positively requires for its fulfilment the recognition of a higher order. Man's life can only be lived on earth successfully if it moves at the same time 'in the heavenly places'.

Surely this is the thought of St. Paul as it would have adapted itself to the twentieth century.

And, indeed, if we ignore the apocalyptic, the prophetic teaching of Christ falls to the ground. Unless it *is* true that the life of man on earth has constant reference to another order in which alone 'true joys are to be found', then He cannot be acquitted of having added to the misery of blind and suffering humanity.[1] He has robbed us of our world and given us no other. 'What have we to do with Thee, Jesus of Nazareth? Hast Thou come hither to torment us?' It needs that sterner and more frightening strain—we may recognize it in all reverence—before His more homely teaching will make sense. The teaching of Christ is supernatural, or it has no message for daily life at all.

But it is undeniable that His teaching, and, indeed, the whole of the New Testament, does unhesitatingly declare that the centre of gravity for human life is to be sought in an eternal Order. So men to-day are discovering afresh the practical truth of the Christian assertion. We are being forced to recognize that Liberty, Fraternity, and Equality are ultimately spiritual problems. Our Lord came into a Society which was eager for a revolution. His contemporaries were longing for release from political tyranny. They were crying out for a new social justice, a fuller freedom, and a richer fellowship. He declared that the preliminary to a renewal of society was a spiritual revolution. He was crucified because men wanted the first, and were not prepared to purchase it by the second. This man or Barabbas? We have still to decide. Christ and Barabbas both desired to see the social order turned upside-down. Barabbas tried to secure his aims by murder: Christ did secure His by being crucified. The same issue confronts the world to-day.

The lasting contribution of St. Paul's thought is that it does put life on its proper stage. He sees society, not as two-dimensional, but as having its explanation in another world. Our citizenship is in heaven, so far as it is effective citizenship. All the time he considers human

[1] This sentence is a reminiscence of a magnificent passage in Bevan's *Hellenism and Christianity*, p. 84.

life as wrapped about with eternal issues. This Epistle starts by regarding human life *sub specie eternitatis.* His thought ranges through the 'heavenly places'—that Eternal Order in which the aspirations and hopes of man are guaranteed in God. So, at the end, he returns to the same theme. They are challenged, he says, with no merely this-world difficulties. They wrestle not merely against flesh and blood, but against the World-rulers of this darkness, the supra-human forces of evil who (as St. Paul believed with his contemporaries) people, unseen, the space between earth and heaven. The drama moves in a more than temporal setting. And that, after all, is the grandeur of man's life, that all the unseen order is committed to the struggles of the individual soul. When the little greengrocer round the corner comes face to face with a temptation, there Michael and his angels shock in battle against the hosts of darkness. Wherever the battle of human life is fought, there is involved also a 'war in heaven'. When the battle is won, there is joy in the presence of the angels of God. The supernatural permeates the natural, and it is impossible to separate them if you wish the life of man to make sense.

It is from the height of this great argument that the New Testament deals with our practical problems.

Wherefore remember, that aforetime ye, the Gentiles in the flesh, who are called Uncircumcision by that which is called Circumcision, in the flesh, made by hands; that ye were at that time separate from Christ, alienated from the commonwealth of Israel, and strangers from the covenants of the promise, having no hope and without God in the world. But now in Christ Jesus ye that once were far off are made nigh in the blood of Christ. For he is our peace, who made both one, and brake down the middle wall of partition, having abolished in his flesh the enmity, *even* the law of commandments *contained* in ordinances; that he might create in himself of the twain one new man, *so* making peace; and might reconcile them both in one body unto God through the cross, having slain the enmity thereby: and he came and preached peace to you that were far off, and peace to them that were nigh: for through him we both have our access in one Spirit unto the Father. So then ye are no more strangers and sojourners, but ye are fellow-citizens with the saints, and of the household of God, being built upon the foundation of the apostles and prophets, Christ Jesus himself being the chief corner stone; in whom each several building, fitly framed together, groweth into a holy temple in the Lord; in whom ye also are builded together for a habitation of God in the Spirit.—Eph. ii. 11–22.

CHAPTER IV

THE HISTORICAL BACKGROUND

'He is our peace, who made both one, and brake down the middle wall of partition.'—Eph. ii. 14.

St. Paul was one of the most profound of thinkers. He was, perhaps, the greatest mind in the West between Aristotle and Michael Angelo. The modern reader must therefore be prepared to find that it needs a good deal of effort fully to assimilate his ideas, at least in his more speculative passages. The early Church seems to have found it, too. 'Our beloved brother Paul,' says the writer of the Letter which goes by the name of '2 Peter', 'writes in all his letters some things that are hard to understand, which ignorant people pervert to their own loss.' [1] Indeed, a good many of his contemporaries very likely regarded St. Paul's Epistles with the same uncomprehending admiration with which to-day a village congregation hears a sermon by an Oxford Don. But he would have indignantly repudiated the suggestion that his thought was academic. He is quite sure that he is dealing with facts, and it is to facts all the time that he appeals. The essential subject-matter of this Epistle is no elaboration of his brain: it is something that has already happened. The new Society was there. It was already in existence. The great decisive act had been performed and the astonishing new thing had appeared. He is not theorizing: he is pointing to something which every one with eyes could see. So, as though to meet an unspoken objection that he was merely handling pretty theories, he comes to earth at the end of the great passage in which he had soared at the close of chap. i, to deal with the actual facts of the situation. 'You were dead in your failures and your sins, but you know your-

[1] 2 Pet. iii. 16.

selves what God has done to make a difference in your lives. Remember that you Gentiles were at that time apart from Christ, in the world without hope and without God; but now, in Christ, the change has been wrought in you.' The thing was actually experienced long before it came to be explained.

And this is, as every one will recognize, the course of all theological development. The religion came first, and theology came later. Christianity did not first appear in the world as a system of beliefs: it was first known as a new way of life. The earliest name for the new faith is 'The Way'. It was tested and verified in action long before it became a philosophy. Later, the imperious necessity of relating religion to the rest of experience drove men to examine what was implied in it, to try and explain what it was that had happened to them, and to state it in terms of a body of thought-out doctrine. And one of the reasons, Mr. T. R. Glover says, why Christianity overcame the Old World was that it was able to outthink it. But it is a matter of first-rate importance to realize the order of this development. For this will save us from misusing the New Testament in a way which is still not wholly obsolete. We must understand that the New Testament is not meant as a text-book of theology, still less as an armoury of 'proof-texts' to be quoted in the interests of orthodoxy. It is primarily the story of an experience, of what God did in the lives of men and women, with some of the first attempts to explain what had happened. It is not a text-book of theology; for it contains, in germ and embryo, three or four different theological systems. It is rather the record, white-hot out of experience, of the concrete, living religious material out of which later generations formulated the body of Christian Doctrine. It is not true to say that the Church was built on the doctrine of the New Testament: the Church was there long before its documents. The New Testament presupposes the life of the Church, and takes for granted as its axiom the common body of Christian experience. The good news had been proved and found valid in the life of the Society long before it was stated as a creed. So here, the Fellowship of the Catholic Church, which stirs St. Paul to these flights of imagination, was a strong and vivid reality years before its basis was stated in words, or the theory upon which it rested analysed. Men who were 'far off' had been brought 'near', long before they attempted explanations of *how* this had been done 'by the Blood of Christ'.

St. Paul deliberately appeals to the historical background of his theory, and it may be useful here to give an outline of it. We will make an attempt to state, very shortly, what it was that had actually been done, and what sort of needs had actually been met, by the organization of the Pauline Churches. We will first try to show, in a few sentences, the main problems of the Roman world into which the new religion came, and notice how closely it is paralleled with what we have said of the need of our own day. The reader not in possession of the facts will find them summarized by the late Prof. Haverfield in Peake's one-volume 'Commentary'[1]—a necessity to every instructed Christian—or, more fully, in two brilliant chapters in Lake's and Jackson's *Beginnings of Christianity*.[2]

Briefly, then, what the Church achieved was to supply the Empire with a soul. Rome had made the greatest experiment before the Commonwealth of British peoples in the organization of a world-state. Alexander the Great and his successors had succeeded in unifying the Near East on the basis of a common culture, transcending, at least to a large extent, the more acute racial distinctions. Rome unified a larger area on the basis of a common law. It had not supplied it with a common emotion or with an adequate stock of common ideas. It is often said that the fall of the Roman Empire was due to the absence of scientific frontiers. The vast land-frontier of the Rhine and Danube was too long to be defended without relying on the subject peoples who ultimately proved the cause of its downfall. This no doubt is true so far as it goes: but we must admit that the question

[1] T. C. and E. C. Jack (12*s*. 6*d*.).

[2] Part I, *The Acts*; vol. i, *Prolegomena* (Macmillan).

goes much deeper than the merely military problem. In one sense, the Empire was too small: it ought to have included Germany. But in another sense it was far too big, though from a more than military standpoint. It was far too big to be adequately organized by the moral resources at its disposal. The wide area of civilization had no corresponding depth. In all outward things the world was one, as it had never been before, and has never been since right up to the Twentieth Century. Outwardly and in all external ways, there was a uniform type of civilization extending from Chester to Cappadocia. Everywhere was the same type of architecture, the same manner of life, the same law and, increasingly, the same language. It is highly significant to notice that, literally, all roads led to Rome. They were not for travel between the different provinces, but to join the provinces with Rome. These magnificent highways linked the capital with all the outlying parts of the Empire. The police system was efficient, and universal travel was safe and rapid as it never was again until modern times. Old tribal and racial distinctions were almost completely obliterated. There has never been a more cosmopolitan age. But it was a world without variety much more than a world that can be called a unity. All the machinery was there, and it was extraordinarily effective, but it lacked the one thing needful. The Romans disregarded the soul of the Empire. They had no real interest in education, and they tended to 'make a tool of religion'. It is true, no doubt, that there was throughout the Empire free universal education: but education by now was mainly rhetoric, that is, it was education in appearances, and left untouched the thing that really mattered. It was left in the hands of Greeks and other slaves, and it made no genuine attempt to organize social emotion or to train the individual to take his place in the community. And it had no common stock of moral ideas. 'Education', as H. G. Wells has written, 'is the preparation of the individual for the community, and his religious training is the core of that preparation.'[1] The Roman Empire

[1] *Outline of History*, p. 602.

could not hold together without the unifying force and the inner dynamic of religion.

Just for a moment it seemed about to find it. The restoration of peace to a torn world when Augustus brought the Civil Wars to a close did inspire men for a few years with a sort of religious emotion towards the Empire. Vergil's feeling is obviously sincere, and we know that in the Eastern Provinces Caesar-worship was a spontaneous growth, the expression of an oriental gratitude to one who had proved himself the world's saviour. Subsequent Caesars decided to 'establish' it, so that religion became a tool of Imperialism, and was thereby at once robbed of its vitality. The old religions were fast losing their hold—though perhaps not so entirely as is sometimes taken for granted. In the fifth century, popular paganism was still strong enough for St. Augustine to think it worth his while to train all his batteries upon it. But to whatever extent it still endured amongst the lower classes of society, it is clear that this old creed of nature-polytheism could supply no moral basis for a world-state. The strongest force making for righteousness was, no doubt, the Stoic philosophy, whose professors were now performing functions closely akin to those of the modern clergyman.[1] And Stoicism taught a splendid doctrine about the City of Zeus, the Kingdom of Mind, transcending all distinctions and divisions, in which all men were at one as citizens in virtue of their common reason. But it is doubtful if this went much farther than the intellectual internationalism of science and letters at the present day. It had no meaning except for the cultured classes. Thus, the great mass of the population, without any common religious inspiration, without any common intellectual life, had no vital unifying force. The world was beginning to learn a new language when the Christian missionaries spoke to it about 'the unity of the Spirit'. The Church did what the Empire failed to do. It began to supply all classes in the Empire with a common spiritual experience and a common moral education. Constantine recognized the situation, and

[1] Inge, in *The Legacy of Greece*, p. 33.

handed over to the Church what Caesar had not succeeded in accomplishing. The sincerest compliment paid to the Christian Church was Julian's attempt at an imitation. The Church did create a civilization, a new spiritual unity, which survived all the shocks of the Barbarians, and held Europe to some extent together, at least until the end of the Middle Ages. *Nostrum, nostrum est imperium Romanum,* wrote Sylvester II to Otto III. So true was this—so completely had the Church inherited all that was enduring in the great experiment of the Roman Empire—that the Holy Roman Empire and the Church came to be indissolubly connected in the European imagination. Men went on believing in the Holy Empire long after it had ceased to be a reality, because it was bound up with the Catholic Church, and apart from the Catholic Church they were unable to conceive that civilization could mean anything.

We will now attempt to describe the evolution of this astonishing experiment. St. Paul, the wise master-builder, did succeed, whether consciously or not, in building up a new civilization within the framework of the old. It is pointed out in all the commentaries, and most effectively by Professor Ramsay, that St. Paul did definitely regard himself as the apostle of the Roman Empire, confining himself strictly within its limits, and travelling mainly along its arterial roads. It might almost seem that he was purposely seeking to endow it with a soul. At any rate, his consummate generalship had an unfailing eye for strategy, and from the day he began his Christian ministry he seems, by a kind of unerring instinct, to have seen how the Cross would succeed where the Eagles failed. It is familiar ground, but it is worth while to spend a few moments in estimating again his magnificent achievement.

The story of his missionary travels and the foundation of his Churches is familiar to everybody from the *Acts.* The narrative need not be repeated here. It is more important to try and get some idea of what it was, in fact, that he was doing. And it comes to this: he was giving conscious unity to the highly heterogeneous elements in the lower strata of the population. He was building up a vigorous corporate life, informed by a common religious inspiration, in the great cosmopolitan centres of the Empire. Jews and Greeks, Romans, Thracians, Dacians, slaves and free men, coloured men and white men, people of all religions or of none, educated and illiterate, who jostled one another in the streets of the great towns like Ephesus and Corinth, suddenly found themselves one family, actuated by one purpose, bound by a new and higher allegiance, bought with a price by one common Redeemer. They were made one man in Christ Jesus. They were bound together in new social contacts, entrusted with new mutual obligations, submitting together to a new moral discipline. Nor must we overlook the high importance of the directly educational work which the Church achieved in her public worship, Bible-study, preaching and catechism. As with the Methodists in the Nineteenth Century, the Christian meetings supplied the training ground for a self-governing democracy.[1] This new unity of spirit changed the complexion of the whole of life and revolutionized men's moral outlook. It created at once a new terminology. 'The Greek words which we translate "joy", "peace", "hope", "humility", are no part of the stock-in-trade of Greek moralists before Christ. Men do not coin new words for old ideas.'[2] The new spiritual relationship in which men began to stand to one another was destined to change the whole face of society. Of this we shall speak more fully in Chapter VII.

Taken as a whole, then, we may say that each of the Churches founded by St. Paul represented a wholly new achievement in the organization of social life. But that would not, in itself, have given unity to the larger world of Imperial civilization. They might, indeed, have proved disruptive forces, as was later to be the case with national Churches. But St. Paul did not regard the matter thus. He did not start with a number of local societies and devise a means of holding them together. He started

[1] Cf. Hammond, *Town Labourer*, chap. xiii.
[2] Inge, in *The Legacy of Greece*, p. 42.

they could not hope to find salvation, St. Paul flung himself against their theory with all the ardour of his passionate nature. Men, as he saw, were brought into the Fellowship along divers ways of experience, and to try to force them all into one mould was to doubt the resourcefulness of God and to fetter the creations of His Spirit. 'As every man has been called, so let him abide.' If a man had been brought up as a Jew, in the thought and experience of the Old Testament, he would obviously express the new faith in totally different language and forms of worship from one brought up in the Greek Mysteries, or a bovine Saxon slave from Britain. To deny the right of local autonomy was, to him, to resist the Spirit of God. Yet he did not allow this local freedom to imperil the conscious fundamental unity which embodied itself in all the parts. For, in his view, what gave the Church its unity and preserved the continuity of its life, was not any singularity of form but the presence of a Risen Life within it. My body is continually changing. It remains 'my' body because it is the organ of my personal continuity: not because it always looks the same or always behaves in the same way. So it is, St. Paul would have said, with the Body of Christ. Our own Hooker's thesis recognized this—'The Church being a body which dieth not hath power as occasion requireth no less to ordain that which never was than to ratify what hath been before.'[1]

The organization of the ministry symbolized and assisted this conception of unity subsisting in variety. There was, as we know now, a double ministry. There were the colleges of presbyters, which developed later into the episcopate, controlling and organizing the local churches. These presbyters derived their commission from himself, on behalf of the whole Church, and were therefore never merely congregational; but they were, at the same time, essentially rulers and ministers of the local Churches. There was also the higher, itinerant ministry—the 'apostles and prophets' of the New Testament—representing the Great Church in its corporate

[1] *Ecclesiastical Polity*, V. xxxv. 3.

aspect, and moving about from one local Church to another.[1] So that there was a constant mutual intercourse between the Church in its catholic idea and the local bodies in which that idea was expressed. The presbyterate, which derived from the apostles, and the episcopate which grew out of it, were the symbols of an enduring unity in which each individual Christian knew himself to be a participator, finding his own individuality in a Fellowship which he did not make—which rather made him, but did not overwhelm him. This was something utterly unique in the history of the human race.

The experiment was magnificently successful. By the second century, at any rate, the average Christian had come to regard himself as a member of a new Fellowship coterminous with, but different from, the world. 'Christians', said one of them in a public tract, 'are not different from the rest of mankind in country or language or customs. They do not live in special cities of their own. They do not speak a peculiar dialect or practise any social idiosyncracies. They live in Greek or Barbarian cities according as each man's lot has fallen to him. They follow the customs in which they were brought up in dress and diet, and other ways of life. And yet in a marvellous and admittedly startling way they show forth the constitution of their own Commonwealth. They live in their own countries, but are there as pilgrims. They share in everything as citizens, and yet submit to everything as aliens. Every foreign land is their country, yet every country a foreign land to them. They pass their time upon the earth, but their citizenship is in heaven. . . . They are attacked by the Jews and persecuted by the Greeks as belonging to another race, yet those who hate them can give no reason for their hostility. In one word, *what the soul is to the body, that Christians are to the world.* The soul extends through all the limbs of the body: so do Christians through all the cities of the world. The soul has its habitation in the body but yet it is not of the body: so Christians have

[1] On all this see Headlam's *Bampton Lectures*, chap. ii, with references.

cover it all in oblivion. There is, no doubt, the appeal of heroic courage in this proud though melancholy creed, but it is in the end a creed of sheer despair; and suicide is its logical conclusion, as the story of ancient Stoicism shows. To rely only on a 'God within' is to lean on a reed which will pierce your hand and then break. The fundamental need for religion is to establish a relationship between the best man knows in his own heart and the nature of Reality itself. There can be nothing but disillusionment in a life dedicated to ideals, unless the universe itself affirms them, unless man's hopes are guaranteed in God. Otherwise, faith is at the mercy of facts. No doubt, when they heard about the Crucifixion, the worldly-wise observed that it proved their point: 'These dreamers always follow a will-o'-the-wisp, but the facts of life break them in the end. So all these idealists must fail. See to what an end he has come, he and his wonderful kingdom of golden dreams.' And, indeed, if that had been the end, there is, I think, no warrant for believing that Love is the truth about the universe. That faith could hardly face the challenge of facts. But it was not the end. God raised Him from the dead, vindicating by that signal act the claims which Jesus made upon the universe. Christ staked His life to show that Love is true, and the Resurrection proved that He was right. It is this which gives us 'boldness towards God', knowing that the Will behind the world is one which guarantees what Christ asserted. So that the whole hope of Christianity in its proclamation of world-fellowship rests irrevocably on the Resurrection. Thus St. Paul, at the opening of this letter in which he seeks to unfold the eternal purpose for uniting all nations in one Body, throws the whole weight of his emphasis on the Resurrection of the Master, as proving that the great plan could be achieved. People could know the hope to which they were called, because of 'the energy of the might of God's power which He energized in Christ when He raised Him from the dead and set Him up above every name that is named, not only in this world but in the world to come'.[1] There was

[1] Chap. i. 18–22.

the charter of the Great Society in which Christ was to come to His fulfilment (i. 23).

But that was where the old religions failed. Mithraism, for example, the severest competitor of Christianity, did set forth in a high and inspiring fashion the hope that men might triumph over circumstances, that through death they might pass into newness of life, that by participating in a mystic sacrifice they could be inheritors of a fuller fellowship. But there was no Mithras and there had been no sacrifice. And Christianity overcame its rivals, not because all its ideals were better than theirs, but because it offered actual facts and was grounded in the historic personality of One who lived and taught and died and rose at a given point in human history, 'in the fifteenth year of the reign of Tiberius Caesar, when Annas and Caiaphas were high-priests.'

There is a tendency to-day to think the fact that a suggestion 'works' is a guarantee enough of its truth. Let us recognize that all suggestions 'work': what we need is a standard by which to test their truth. Mithraism and the Mysteries and many far less reputable religions succeeded admirably with their suggestions; for that we have unmistakeable evidence. But the Christian case as against them is, partly, this—that Christianity has objective reasons for asserting that its suggestions are *true*.

The Church has always known, with unerring instinct, that to weaken men's hold on the historic facts is to weaken their hold on the Christian view of life. The whole of Christian philosophy as an interpretation of the universe rests unalterably on the conviction that the eternal Mind which informs the world came forth and manifested itself to human experience at a given point in time and space. But if so, if in the earthly life of Jesus there was a breaking-through of the eternal Order, then not only are historic facts supremely important in the Christian scheme, but also the facts of that historic Life will supply the key to interpret the whole process. No one can take the Incarnation seriously without attempting in some form or other what we now call a 'philosophy of history'. If it be true that God became flesh, then, at that concrete moment in interpreting the Old Testament, had employed what to us is a rather difficult notion, that the first Adam in the Garden of Eden had, somehow, contained within himself all the human race that sprang from him. St. Paul was quick to cap this speculation with his doctrine of the Second Adam. As, in the ancestor of a sinful race, all its failure, strife, and sorrow had been, as they held, contained in one individual, so in the Second Adam sent by God were gathered up all human possibilities. And it was, as he says in *Ephesians*, the purpose of God to 'recapitulate' all things in this Man, the Christ.[1]

It is, no doubt, some such idea as this which has led theologians to maintain that Jesus Christ was not *a* man, but Man. Strictly speaking, of course, this is nonsense. There is clearly no such thing as Manhood which is not the manhood of individual men. But it is easy enough to understand the religious values they were trying to guard; and an easy illustration comes to our aid. There is a sense, for example, in which Shakespeare seems to have entered into the experience of the whole range of human life: there is hardly a secret of the human heart which his mind seems not to have understood. One might say, using loose and popular language, 'William Shakespeare cannot be called a man: he is Elizabethan England.' Yet we know all the time that he was an intensely concrete, individual person. But this is the kind of thing that St. Paul and later theologians have intended, in speaking of Christ as the Representative Man. They meant that there is no human experience into which He has not completely entered, and that there are no human possibilities which He has not triumphantly fulfilled. In Him we see what human nature means.

This gives us a kind of clue which holds together the profoundest utterances of Christian Doctrine. And this is, roughly, what St. Paul is saying when he declares that the mystery of God's will, purposed in Him to be worked out in the fullness of the time, is visible now before the eyes of men; and that the eternal purpose, purposed in Christ before the worlds were made, was now being

[1] Eph. i. 10.

revealed in the Church. We can see what He means. As he looks back now over the issues of his crowded years of active life, watching the growth of this new fellowship which was cutting across the most forbidding distinctions, welding the most recalcitrant material into a new and undreamed-of unity, and recognizing there the operation of the Spirit of the historic Christ, he sees in a flash that the whole of human history is coming to its consummation there. The mystery of the ages has now been revealed by the Spirit. He longs to proclaim to a bewildered world what is the true hope of men's calling—the possibility of world-wide Fellowship which has always been the purpose of God's will. Fellowship was God's eternal purpose, purposed before the foundation of the world. In the emergence of this new Society, the direct result of the life and death of Jesus, the creative purpose was coming to its fulfilment. These queer little commonwealths of despised and often disreputable people were the culmination of God's plan. These, the flotsam and jetsam of the human race, whom St. Paul had organized into his local churches, were, after all, no mere by-products of an evolutionary process. They were the objects of an eternal plan, a purpose always at work in history, flaming out into palpable form and shape in the Life that was lived in Palestine and the society which that Life created. Here, he saw, was that purpose 'reserved for the fullness of the times, purposed in Christ before the worlds were made', coming to its fruition in Jesus of Nazareth. This new and irresistible Fellowship was no mere accident of history, but the mature achievement of the Divine Will. These people to whom he writes his letter had been called by God from the foundation of the world.

That is to say, there is guiding the course of the world a Purpose which is a will to Fellowship. The mysterious processes of 'selection' which, when in earlier days he wrote the *Romans*, had caused Paul such perplexity of mind, now fell into their place in the scheme of things. One had been taken and another left, the Jew chosen, not the more capable Greek, the Jew rejected now and the Gentile called. But this principle of selectiveness in history,

Divinity of Christ. For it is the only safeguard against a dualism which reduces our experience to nonsense. If Christ were admitted to be the highest expression of the spirit of man, or the divine Spirit in man, but not of the Will that controls the natural order, then there remains a hopeless contradiction in any attempt to harmonize our thinking. There remain two principles in *opposition* with no possibility of a bridge between. This—the essentially oriental tendency—has always been recognized by the Christian Church as its most insidious enemy. It has threatened the Church in many different forms, and has every time been instinctively resisted. There is no doubt that to superficial thinking it does provide an attractive short way out from the pressing burden and challenge of the Universe. To worship a God whom we know in the heart, and to leave the order of nature to unknown forces, gives, at first sight, at least some ground to stand upon in a world so baffling and hard to understand. But, on reflection, it leaves the natural order as a non-moral process altogether. Huxley was prepared for this conclusion. But the life of men is then unliveable. For *the* most certain fact of human experience—the fact of moral struggle and aspiration—is then admittedly a mere delusion. For the moral life has then to be expressed in an order which—on the basis of this position—is ever impervious to moral principles. There is no sense to be made of life in this way. Christ is merely a mocker of men's misery. He can have no significance for men unless He is the expression and embodiment of the Purpose informing the whole universe with which our experience brings us into contact. That is what Christians mean by the assertion that He must be nothing less than 'God from God'.

This attempted escape by the way of dualism has been revived in our time by Mr. Wells. In *The Undying Fire,* and in other books, Mr. Wells conceives a young Christ-like God who is known and worshipped in the heart of man, but has no necessary connexion with the overlord of Nature. Why this idea is religiously unsatisfying I have tried to suggest in the preceding paragraph. I would add a consideration from philosophy. The result of Mr. Wells's metaphysics, if pressed to their logical conclusion, is a proof that science is impossible—a curious position for a scientist. For the whole success of scientific inquiry presupposes that the natural order is knowable by the human mind—i. e. that there is within it or behind it a rational principle or mind akin to the human mind of the researcher. Admit this cleavage into our philosophy, and the natural order with which science deals becomes for ever opaque to the mind of man. This theory, in fact, is but Kant turned upside down. God is known; and the whole order of nature, over which hitherto man's mind has claimed dominion, is relegated to the Unknowable. This will hardly be thought to be very satisfying. Evolution cannot be explained if it moves in this way along two parallel lines—one towards a non-moral Nature, the other to Man, reaching towards God. There is no common principle: they never meet.

But the Christian lives without fear in the world because he knows himself at home in it. For it is, as Jesus said, his Father's world. The Christ who has shown him God in human life, has shown him also the Spirit who made the world. The 'Divinity of Christ' involves for us that the realm of nature and the realm of spirit both proceed from the same controlling Will. Christ has revealed the meaning of creation. It is odd that Christian thinkers have been so slow to see that loyalty to science and history are essentially bound up with the 'Nicene' orthodoxy.

Armed with this key we can unlock the secret. In the light of Christ the story does make sense. And if, as the methods of science would require of us, we seek an explanation of the world in terms of this, the highest that we know of it, we find in fact clear traces of this same purpose which St. Paul set forth in this glowing piece of writing. For, indeed, the key to the story of evolution is not cruelty but altruism. Not only is it clear that self-sacrifice, the surrender of the individual for the fulfilment of the racial life, is the dominant fact in the whole process. It is also clear that the story of civilization is the story of wider fellowship. He could not, or he would not, venture out on to the path of wider co-operation. He did not obey the laws which govern life. He, too, dashed himself against the Rock, and the Jewish nation-state had to perish at last lest the path to fellowship should be obstructed.

But, indeed, right across the highway of the Spirit has stood this barrier of Privilege. The Greeks said openly what many people still believe in their secret hearts to-day, that there were some people who are 'by nature slaves', born to positions of inferiority and to be exploited by the privileged class. What the Greek believed of slavery, the Jew believed in the sphere of religious truth. But no privilege of any kind, religious, economic, or political, is tolerable to Christian thought. Whenever the proclamation of Christianity has been true to its own genius, privilege has trembled on its throne. 'He has put down the mighty from their seat and has exalted the humble and meek.' The forces of privilege and reaction have always recognized in Christ the greatest menace that ever threatened them. The magistrates of the Empire were quite right in regarding Christianity as treason. It was. For Imperial society was a society of privilege. Its magnificence and splendour, the ruins of which still strike the imagination so stupendously all over Europe, were built over a great gulf that yawned between the few who were admitted to them and the great mass of the disinherited. To that society, as to all others like it, the new religion acted as a solvent. For Christ had brought the perilous doctrine of a spiritual democracy based on equality in the sight of God, in which there can be neither Jew nor Greek, privileged nor unprivileged, white or coloured, bond or free. And it is only in such a fellowship, the true expression of the eternal Purpose, that the meaning of human life can be understood. You can only see what man is meant to be when the life of man is organized by the Spirit. 'The student of plant life could never deduce from his knowledge of vegetables the possibility of animals. The zoologist could not predict human civilization and Art and Religion from his acquaintance with animal existence. We never know what matter is capable of till we see life in possession: we never know what either matter or life is capable of till we see Spirit in control of both. Man reveals the possibilities of the lower ranks of creation. In the same way we could not have known what humanity is capable of, if God had not once lived a human life.' [1]

The Spirit of God is the Spirit that wills fellowship, and the individual only enters into the meaning of his human life when he is caught up into a Fellowship in which he can rise above his limitations, finding himself in the fullness of the whole. In such a group he rises above himself. For the Fellowship created by the Spirit is human life at its highest and most intense, a society most completely organized and therefore offering fullest scope for all the capacities of the individual. Again, at this point, we find help in recent writing. Dr. MacDougall has shown, in *The Group Mind*, that in a simple and unorganized 'crowd' the individual is lowered to a moral and intellectual level far inferior to his own. In a highly organized group, on the other hand, the average moral and intellectual level is higher than that of the individual.[2] By identifying himself with such a group the individual transcends himself and reaches a level of thought and capacity which would be otherwise beyond his grasp. So it is with that organic life of the Spirit which St. Paul calls 'the Body of Christ'. In it all the barriers are down. In it there are open to each one the treasures of the fullness of the whole; and, as he loses himself in that society which transcends all privilege and all distinctions, a man begins to realize the possibilities of human nature when it is informed by the Spirit of God. You are, St. Paul had said, 'Body-of-Christ' (1 Cor. xii. 27).

NOTE

There appears to be a growing agreement in the scientific world that the claim of mere natural selection to be the decisive factor in evolution cannot be any

[1] W. Temple, in *The Pilgrim*, Jan. 1921, p. 228.
[2] *The Group Mind*, chaps. i. and ii.

longer maintained. A striking confirmation, from a biological point of view, of the argument I have developed in this chapter may be found in a paper (' Evolution at the Crossways ') by Mr. H. Reinheimer in *Psyche*, July 1922, from which I am allowed to quote extracts.[1]

' Now this inter-dependence of the organs is the very thing just now to arouse the wonderment of physiologists. They have been forced to the conclusion that what happens at one place of the body is in consonance with what is occurring at another, that, in fact, every part acts more distinctly for the good of the whole than for its own advantage. In other words, modern physiology reveals a kind of physiological or bio-morality. For it is usually recognized that moral action consists in the renunciation of personal gratifications for the sake of a social end. If the parts fail duly to co-operate, then disease and inferiority inevitably ensue.

' Physiology is driven to the recognition of the " law of the members ", although many scientists hesitate to admit the fact, lest they be accused of metaphysics. They fight shy of an approximation to religious views, as though these were not often based merely on scientific experience. Science is afraid of receiving back its own at the hands of religion—an attitude for which, of course the obscurantism, which, we all hope, is of the past, has to be blamed.

' With the advance of modern physiology, then, co-operation is increasingly coming into its own. But Nature knows no watertight compartments. Not only is it true that organs are semi-independent organisms, co-operating " at home " ; they also co-operate " abroad ". That is to say, organs and organisms are involved in a common sociality, are jointly and severally under a basic law of concord. There is no " pure " physiology, i.e. a science of the relations of the parts, which could be interpreted exclusively in physico-chemical terms. Invariably there is an important admixture of sociology. The work of the organism may be finally based upon

[1] By kind permission of Messrs. Kegan Paul, Trench, Trübner & Co., Ltd.

chemical energy. But this chemical energy is directed by something else which is not itself a chemical energy, and which is associated with the organic synthesis which that energy serves to maintain. Physiology and sociology are eternally inseparable. They form an indissoluble amalgam.

'Hence the need for a socio-physiological science, involving a simultaneous study of sociological and related physiological and biological activities together with recognition of values in the results of these activities. Socio-physiology will bring into rational unity physiological phenomena with those appertaining to the interdependence of life. It alone is competent to deal at all comprehensively with the evolutionary problem.

'Had there not been a serious and unavoidable hiatus in Darwin's theory on the score of socio-physiology, he would have had fewer difficulties with the problem of extinction, regarding which he frankly declared himself puzzled. Millions of species in the past have done all that could be required of them according to natural selection. Had they not "struggled", changed, and become "adapted"? Had they not become formidable and even, for a time, "successful"? Yet they ended dismally, whilst others kept on flourishing.

'The suspicion naturally arising that the failing species had transgressed against sociological law, that they have lived illegitimately at the price of future ruin, is hardly to be resisted, although it may be rejected as "metaphysics"—a counsel of despair—by those who have no alternative view.

'Darwin at least surmised that liability to extinction may be due to "lack of improvement according to the principle of the all-important relations of organism to organism in the struggle for life".

'This is at any rate a faint adumbration of the view that bad behaviour is the source of the evil, and, as such, it is certainly an advance on natural selection. It is a suggestion of a vital, though mysterious, element of progress contained in "mutual relations". Lack of this vital element spells inferiority and disease. Somehow (to continue Darwin's visualization of a great socio-physiological truth) the organism has to be fruitful in its relations with others, lest it forfeit its place in life. Stability, efficiency, and permanence depend upon a satisfactory relatedness, whatever it may be, to the web of life. The organic world seems to go forward as a whole. Hence all organisms are under necessity to maintain a respective social nexus on pain of being estranged from inter-connected, inter-determined, progess and thus rendered liable to extinction.

'That such or similar considerations were not at all foreign to Darwin's mind, may be inferred from his other suggestion that the diversification of organisms in a given district had much the same advantages as the division of labour in the body, which, as we now see, is a monument to co-operation. So he pointed out that "after long intervals of time, the productions of the world seem to have changed simultaneously"—another hint at inter-connected progress.

'Can it be true, after all, that the cardinal necessity of life is not so much for the organism to fit itself merely expediently to any and every condition, but rather to strive towards the achievement of the purpose of life by obedience to some sublime law of inter-dependence and of inter-determination ? That a life aiming merely at self-sufficiency receives no encouragement from Nature ?

'The writer fully believes that this is so. He has designated the respective progressive principle of evolution : Symbiogenesis, by which he means the direction given to evolution by the long-continued operation of Symbiosis in the production of higher forms of life, and in the more complete development of beneficial relations between them. Obedience to this law is more important in progressive evolution than mere adaptation. The adaptability of protoplasm is a necessary condition of evolution ; but when the organism degenerates as a whole, we are driven to conclude that in the majority of cases when the organism fails apparently as a result of mechanical or similar obstacles it encounters, these obstacles have not been duly provided against on the psychical side. The cause of failure, in other words, resolves itself into this: transgression of the law of co-operation, of reciprocity, of compensation—in short, a divorce from Symbiosis. *Res nolunt diu maleadministrari.*

'By maintaining Symbiosis the organism is apt to draw to itself those "great allies" to which Wordsworth and Emerson alluded: the powers for good implicit in the nature of the world.'

For this cause I bow my knees unto the Father, from whom every fatherhood in heaven and on earth is named, that he would grant you, according to the riches of his glory, that ye may be strengthened with power through his Spirit in the inward man; that Christ may dwell in your hearts through faith; to the end that ye, being rooted and grounded in love, may be strong to apprehend with all the saints what is the breadth and length and height and depth, and to know the love of Christ which passeth knowledge, that ye may be filled unto all the fulness of God. . . .

I therefore, the prisoner in the Lord, beseech you to walk worthily of the calling wherewith ye were called, with all lowliness and meekness, with longsuffering, forbearing one another in love; giving diligence to keep the unity of the Spirit in the bond of peace. *There is* one body, and one Spirit, even as also ye were called in one hope of your calling; one Lord, one faith, one baptism, one God and Father of all, who is over all, and through all, and in all.—Eph. iii. 14–iv. 6.

Husbands, love your wives, even as Christ also loved the church, and gave himself up for it; that he might . . . present the church to himself a glorious *church*, not having spot or wrinkle or any such thing; but that it should be holy and without blemish. Even so ought husbands also to love their own wives as their own bodies.—Eph. v. 25–8.

CHAPTER VI

FELLOWSHIP AND GROUP-LOYALTY

'The Father, from whom every fatherhood in heaven and on earth is named.'—Eph. iii. 14.

In the last chapter we saw that St. Paul recognizes in the historic life of Christ and the emergence of the Christian Church the key to the meaning of human history. The Purpose that controls the world is, he sees, a Will to fellowship. In Chapter IV of his Letter he takes us further. He shows us the ultimate ground for this assertion. God wills fellowship, because ultimately fellowship *is* the life of God. Jesus has revealed to the world not merely abstract principles in accordance with which life is organized: He has revealed the heart of His Father. The truest and deepest word that can be spoken about the creative Purpose of the universe is, in our Lord's words: 'Our Father'. From Him all fellowship derives, and in the perfection of the divine Life is the archetype of all human fellowship. 'I bow my knees', says St. Paul, 'to the Father from whom all fatherhood (or, every family) both in heaven and on earth derives.'[1] In other words, all true human fellowship is rooted and grounded in the nature of God.

St. Paul thus comes very close here to St. John. 'Where love is', says St. John, 'there is God, and where God is, there is love, because the essential nature of God *is* Love.' So that wherever you have human fellowship, there is the expression in time and space of the eternal life which is in God. To know love is to know God; to 'abide in' love is to 'abide in' God; and to live out of fellowship with men is to be cut off from true knowledge of God. The whole thought of St. John is saturated with this conception of eternal life

[1] The Greek cannot mean, 'the whole family', as A.V.

—which, in the light of the historic Jesus, he knows to be the life of fellowship—penetrating all human relationships and expressing itself recognizably by men in this world that comes to be and passes away.

Thus in this Letter, where the two great streams of Pauline and Johannine thought meet, we are able to pierce to the heart of the situation. The explanation of human society is to be sought in a higher Order. Human society is made possible by the presence of the supernatural. It derives from the eternal Life itself, and is the manifestation of God's life in the relationships of finite spirits. God is the ground of its existence, and apart from Him it cannot come into being. Just as, if we think its implications out, thought implies a 'Thinker' as well as a thinker, so the very conception of society pre-supposes God and eternal life. We can now see why Christianity denies that civilization can be built upon a merely natural foundation. It cannot, because the power of living together is something which only the Spirit of God makes possible; and we cannot adequately conceive society except in so far as our thinking starts from God. This, as we shall see a little later on, is the very antithesis and contradictory of a view which is highly fashionable at present.

Any decent philosophy of the State will find the real ground of society in the social character of personality. Society cannot be rightly regarded as an aggregation of individuals contracting with one another to live together. It is rather to be regarded as the expression of an inner necessity of human life. Man is by nature a social being, and to try to think of man apart from society is to think of something which is not man at all. Thus all psychology is social psychology, and the very conception of personality necessarily includes relation to and intercourse with other human persons. Man has come to be what he is, and will grow up to what he can become, only in and through a social life. This line of thought is now so familiar as to be almost a platitude. But it is clear now that we cannot stop there. Behind this fact there lies a deeper fact. Just in so far as human personality is the expression of the divine Spirit—i. e. as man is made in the image of God—so far the social nature of personality has its roots in the social nature of God. Man must be always striving for fellowship because God's life is perfect fellowship. The most characteristic fact about human nature is rooted and grounded in the Love of God. It is, indeed, logically impossible to conceive the perfection of human personality, unless you start with the conception of a perfect all-containing personality, the underlying ground of finite persons, the objective standard to which they can be referred and the goal to which they continually aspire. Ultimately no psychology and no philosophy of human nature can make sense unless it starts with God. That is, you can only understand the finite by reference to the complete and unconditioned. Or, to put the same thing in common speech, you can only really believe in human nature if your thought is based on faith in God.

Now here, it seems to me, Christianity comes directly into opposition with a certain tendency in the modern world. There is in popular writing nowadays a great deal of very vague thinking about what is loosely called the 'gregarious instinct'. It is taken for granted, without much examination, that in some mysterious and convenient fashion the spontaneous operation of this instinct widening out into ever larger circles will automatically produce the world-state. 'It has created national patriotism: very soon it will lead to internationalism.' This is a new form of the old fallacy which regarded Evolution as necessarily synonymous with Progress. But the facts of history give little warrant to this amiable supposition. The gregarious instinct is no unmixed blessing. Left to itself indeed, and undirected, it rather hinders than advances progress.

Dr. MacDougall has shown that in the modern world its direct operation is apt to produce 'injurious social results' in the over-crowding of the urban areas and the depopulation of the countryside, quite beyond the limits—wide as they are—of real economic necessity.[1] But

[1] *Social Psychology*, 14th ed., p. 301.

there are other obvious illustrations. It is always, for example, bound to be the antagonist of intellectual freedom. Originality is its worst enemy. Resistance to any form of new ideas is a marked feature of all human 'herds'. This is written large across religious history. Institutionalism is always prone to regard 'heresy' as an act of treason far blacker than inconsistency of life. Orthodoxy becomes the test of virtue, and the 'modernist', by whatever name he is called, is hated and persecuted in every age. Each generation stones its prophets—as our Lord said in the most biting of His sayings—and the next builds them martyrs' memorials.[1] Nor is the Church to-day yet emancipated from this obscurantist influence. Some hymns that we sing are full of exhortations to stand together and resist new ideas—like so many cows when a dog comes into the field. Even to-day to call a man a 'modernist' is to most Churchmen a term of personal abuse. It is clear that we have here an example of the social instinct making for reaction. Nor can one see any hope of enlightenment till this instinct is recognized for what it is and so consciously transformed. It should be made clear that the Churchman's loyalty is not—ultimately—to the Church, but to One who claimed to be in Himself the personified and incarnate Truth.

And, again, its crude operation seems to divide men rather than unite them. Just as, by the strange alchemy of nature, the anti-social instinct of pugnacity has become one of the strongest forces by which societies are held together; so, as though to balance this anomaly, the unfettered play of the social instinct has served to organize groups of men in intense hostility to one another. Just in proportion to its intensity it emphasizes the antagonism of the group concerned to all other similar groups. It is only under the solvent of new ideas and the weakening of primitive herd-instinct, that any coalescence is made possible between one group and the others surrounding it. We cannot then look forward with great confidence to the automatic operation of the gregarious instincts of mankind in organizing wider and fuller

[1] Luke xi. 48, Matt. xxiii. 29, 30.

fellowship. So that, while it is true that Christian thinkers striving to lead mankind to a larger unity must give its full value to social psychology, it is equally true that psychology clearly warns us that when the gregarious instinct is left to itself it may prove rather a foe than an ally. From mutually exclusive groups to a larger grouping which shall contain them all there is no path by merely natural processes. The instinct has to be controlled and directed by something that is more than instinct.

Indeed, I would go so far as to maintain that what Christian thought calls 'fellowship' and what psychology calls 'group-loyalty' are at bottom incompatible terms. The very definition of group-loyalty includes antagonism to other groups, and the very definition of fellowship includes the idea of something shared with all. Group-loyalty is essentially self-centred: it is loyalty to the particular group: therefore it is inherently exclusive. But Christian fellowship is God-centred: it is loyalty to the Universal: and therefore it is inherently inclusive. The instrument of group-loyalty is the black ball: that of fellowship is evangelization. No addition of particulars can ever result in a universal. But a universal can and always must express itself through particulars. Christian fellowship, in other words, starts not with the thought of local groups, adding them together into a world-group. It starts with God, whose life is perfect fellowship, manifesting Himself in and through all the relationships of human fellowship. 'That which was from the beginning . . . that eternal life declare we unto you that you may have fellowship with us; and our fellowship is with the Father and with His Son Jesus Christ.'[1] So the concern of Christianity, as a principle of social organization, is with a universal Life of fellowship expressing itself in various degrees through all the hierarchy of lesser loyalties. The universal Spirit organizes and articulates the whole Body. It is not a question of federating groups into a unity which will contain them all. Rather, we say that a pre-existing unity shows itself in and through a rich variety, so that each

[1] 1 John i. 1.

social unit is an expression of that Life which is fellowship. Fellowship on however small a scale is the expression of the divine life gradually coming to fulfilment. And after all, 'an eternal realization of an eternal capacity for fellowship' is very near to the Christian thought of God. There is all the difference in the world between a number of smaller social groups, each of which is the expression of a common Life in which they all partake, and a number of conflicting groups, each of them organized by its own group-loyalty, trying to rise to a larger unity.

The natural basis, it need hardly be said, is the same in each of the two cases. Fellowship no less than group-loyalty operates in and through the herd-instinct. The difference lies in the object or the aim by which the instinctive forces are set in motion. Nor do we seek to deny—we have rather emphasized—that God is at work in that tendency to associate which runs through progressive life on the natural level. The account we should give of it would perhaps be this. All instinct comes from God, that of the herd no less than sex and hunger. And God is the ultimate goal of its development. But instinct leads man home to God again just in proportion as it is 'sublimated' in increasingly spiritual satisfactions. Instinct answers to environment. Now there is, and always has been, a spiritual factor in environment which comes to be gradually apprehended as consciousness slowly develops in range and richness.[1] When Man appears in the story of evolution, then there has come to be present a capacity for conscious response to the spiritual factor. The more clearly and fully this factor is understood, the more distinctively 'human' Man becomes. So we should say that what makes Fellowship is man's innate social disposition when it is consciously evoked in response to a conscious recognition of God. All social life, wherever it may be found, is in its various degrees and levels an expression of God, whose life is Fellowship. From Him every family derives. But it is arrested and baulked of its true development if it stops short of universalism. And this can only come by the recognition of God as the

[1] Cf. McDowall, *Evolution and the Need of Atonement*, pp. 14–20.

Source of all the will to unity, and by consciously entering into relations with Him. Perhaps we can only give the name of Fellowship to the group-life whose centre is God in Christ. Thus natural friendship becomes Christian Fellowship when guided and penetrated by the spirit of Christ. There is genuine Fellowship between friends, or in the social life of a given group, when they love one another, because of Christ in them.

This conception of man's social life as depending on the eternal life of God is diametrically opposed to the fashionable 'group theories' of religion. These theories take a good many different forms, but all agree in the view that belief in God is merely a by-product of the gregarious instinct. In the more elaborate form of this proposition as held by the two well-known French writers, M. Durkheim and M. Lévy Bruhl, it is argued that the mind of primitive man works by processes which they call 'pre-logical', as being bound up entirely with group-consciousness. All religion (they proceed to argue) as being grounded in this social consciousness is therefore in the end mere illusion. Thus religion, as an entirely *social* experience, can be preserved for the individual only so far as he yields himself to the influences of social suggestion and abandons the activity of reason. In the less elaborate form of the same theory as found in several recent English books, it is taken for granted that what plain men call God is only 'a concentrated projection of all the qualities useful to the herd in a supreme supernatural personality, the supreme herd-leader of humanity'.[1] In all these views the tendency is the same, to find in the social nature of religion the proof that it is in the end delusory. As man advances to freedom and wider knowledge this primitive delusion will be eliminated.[2]

Christian thought would be the last to deny the social

[1] Tansley, *New Psychology*, p. 137.

[2] For discussion of these views see Pratt, *Religious Consciousness*, chap. i, criticism in MacDougall's *Group Mind*, chap. iv; Von Hügel's paper, 'Religion and Illusion,' in *Essays and Addresses*; and C. C. J. Webb, *Group Theories of Religion*.

character of religion or its connexion with man's social life. Rather, it emphasizes this to the fullest extent. Only it finds in God not an illusion created by the group-consciousness, but the very explanation of the group. No doubt it is true that the group projects its concepts. No doubt it is true that it often does so in mythology and symbolism, which later ages see to be absurd. But you have still to account for the group being there. The Christian position is that every fellowship is, in its degree, an expression of God's life, though not of course always recognized as such. Just because it is the life of God, it is something which all the groups share in common and through which they can rise to the consciousness of a unity which transcends and includes them all. It is in this way that Christian thought and practice answer the need for a hierarchy of loyalties. Christianity does not seek to organize a world-state by detaching men from their local loyalties, which would be psychologically unsound. It rather regards the local ties and loyalties as the creation of the universal Spirit in virtue of which our citizenship is in Heaven. It regards the family, the city, and nation as at once the school of the larger loyalty and in themselves manifestations of it. It does not want us to be de-naturalized but super-naturalized in the City of God. Any Christian who has really thought out the full meaning of his inheritance in the universal Church will recognize both that through the life of Christ, mediated to him by the Church, he is a member of a Kingdom which transcends all human antagonisms, and also that in the immediate duties of the calling wherewith God has called him he will best discharge the obligation of citizenship in the City which is above.

Such a recovered grip on the significance of what is really implied in 'Churchmanship' would not make men in the wrong sense 'other-worldly'. It would rather cancel the bad division between what is popularly called 'Church-work' and the duties of our home or our profession. The Church conceived in its eternal idea 'can present no other view than that a Christian's whole life is in the Church, whether he is thinking of his home, his business, his social recreations, or his citizenship'.[1] It should not only enrich and sanctify all the associations of human life, bringing them all within the sphere of the Church: it should also offer constantly to the mind of every one of its members the idea of that larger fellowship of which every member of the Church, whatever his colour or language, is a member. And it is, as our psychologists assert, to the liberating influence of ideas that we must look for the broadening of our groupings and the re-direction of the social instinct. 'Just as the minor group sentiments are not incompatible with but rather may strengthen the national sentiment when subordinated to and incorporated in it, so the national sentiment is not incompatible with still more widely inclusive group-sentiments . . . and while loyalty to humanity as a whole is a noble ideal, it is one which can only be realized through a further step in that process of extension of the object of the group sentiment, of which extension patriotism itself is the culmination at present for the great mass of civilized mankind. The attempt to achieve it by any other road is bound to fail because psychologically unsound. . . . The four ideas, liberty, equality, progress, and human solidarity or universal responsibility, seem to be the ideas which in conjunction with national sentiments are more than any other fashioning the future of the world.'[2] It is precisely these four ideas which would be most vividly before men's minds if they realized their membership in the Society of which Christ is the controlling life—the Fellowship of the Christ that is to be. For men's ideas of the goal of human life depend upon their conception of God's nature.

St. Paul himself would seem to be affirming very much what I have suggested here. It cannot be for nothing that the Letter, which opens with the magnificent description of the Church eternal in the Heavens manifesting to the ages to come the manifold wisdom of God's purposes, should end with common-sense work-a-day directions about the conduct of daily life and duty.

[1] Jenks, *The Fulfilment of the Church*, p. 112.
[2] MacDougall, *Group Mind*, pp. 181, 185.

Wives are to serve their husbands in the Lord—'because Christ loved the Church'. The ordinary relationships of the home, between parents and children, servants, masters, and so on, are to be the expression in daily life of their membership in the Catholic Society, 'because we are members of His Body'.[1] This sort of thing, he says, is implied in practice by belonging to the household of the Saints.

It is worth while dwelling on this a little longer. For a richer conception of what is meant by Churchmanship would be the best safeguard against that ecclesiasticism which threatens to choke the life of the Church at present. The religiosity of religious people is one of the worst enemies of religion. It reduces Churchmanship to a sectional interest—something we do in part of our leisure time, certain emotions which are cultivated by people of a certain temperament. It leaves altogether outside the range of religion nearly all the interests and activities which fill the working hours of normal people. But true Churchmanship is the negation of pietism. Christianity in the rich New Testament sense is irreconcilable with pious hobbies. It involves the whole width and range of natural life—its work, its art, its friendships, its amusements—penetrated and transfigured by the presence of the Supernatural.[2] The Bishop of Pretoria made this point clear in the book he wrote just before the Armistice. 'I do not believe that we religious folk commonly have got the right answer ready to the question, What is the will of God for a subaltern? I believe that we should generally answer that he should keep straight; that he should be a good Churchman and go to Communion; that he should be assured of salvation, &c. These answers are partial, for they miss the main thing in a subaltern's life, which is, if he is worth his salt, being a subaltern. The will of God for a subaltern is platoon leading. . . . If a subaltern loves God and gives Him his heart, it is in platoon leading that he is to glorify His Name.'[3]

[1] Eph. iv. 25–vi. 9.
[2] Cf. pp. 39, 40, above.
[3] N. S. Talbot, *Religion behind the Front*, p. 77.

That is exactly, I think, what St. Paul is saying. 'The Church' embraces and operates in and through the normal occupations of daily life. Through them it makes its impact on the world. They are the Church, focussed at that point. After all, it was for most of us through the Church in the person of our parents—in the duties and relationships of home-life—that we came to have any knowledge of Christ at all. Thus Christianity does not imply any peculiar kind of activities. It implies the normal activities of life, each inspired by a different kind of motive.

Each sphere of life must claim its own 'autonomy': but each will be recognized and acknowledged as a province of the whole. Art, for example, will rightly claim to be judged only by strictly aesthetic categories. It cannot, as Art, have any 'ulterior motive'. Once Art attempts to 'preach' or convey a moral, it almost invariably becomes bad art.[1] Art must be understood to be religious simply and wholly by being good art; not by dealing with edifying subjects. People sometimes talk about 'sacred art' as though its sacredness consisted in the subject-matter with which the artist deals. 'Sacred music,' for example, used to be played on Sunday afternoons, while better music, which was considered 'secular' was ruled out, on religious grounds. But this is a radically false standard of judgement. If pressed, it would compel us to maintain that a bad hymn tune is more religious than a Beethoven Sonata or a late Italian Holy Family than the Hermes of Praxiteles.

Tested by such absurd examples the absurdity of the criterion is obvious. We must realize that what makes art religious is simply its own aesthetic perfection as an embodiment of beauty. Suppose that a Rembrandt portrait is rightly judged to be as good art as a fresco by Fra Angelico, then it is equally religious, though the subject has nothing to do with Bible stories. On the other hand, Guido Reni, for example, however much he deals with sacred subjects, produces pietism, not good art. His

[1] This is why Ruskin's criticism is so irritating and Tennyson's poetry sometimes so intolerable.

pictures are far less religious than Rembrandt's portraits or a Corot landscape.

It would be palpably absurd, then, if the Church were to claim the right to establish a censorship over Art and letters. But yet all good art and all true science must be seen to be an expression of the Church—a creation of the Spirit who is her life. Only, they must be given independence. If they forsake their own proper sphere, and substitute the desire to 'edify' for beauty and truth as their sole aim and standard, they are not merely false to themselves. They are being false to the Spirit and the Church. Similarly, if the Church attempted to override their independence, she would be circumscribing her own empire.

Our own mediaeval Church-builders have left us standing witnesses in stone to the inclusiveness of the Great Church. They achieved for mankind in their own artistic sphere what the Schoolmen tried to do in the realm of intellect. Scholasticism was a noble attempt to unify all human knowledge by the light of what Plato called the Form of Good. It sought to correlate all truths of reason by the master-light of God's truth in revelation. Inadequate and even ludicrous as it undeniably became, it deserves our homage as a 'splendid failure'. But it failed, just as the Papacy had failed in its attempt to unify human statesmanship, by its jealousy of independence. It thought that freedom would endanger unity. It was not given to it to understand how unity can subsist within variety. It therefore attempted to control knowledge in the supposed interest of religious truth. The inevitable retribution followed: it became obscurantist and repressive, and men had to break its yoke from their necks if they were to be loyal to the truth. The revolt was in itself a religious movement. No one would deny that there was in the Renaissance a revolt against Christian morality and religion and a cult of what we call neo-Paganism. It infected the papal court very deeply. But the intellectual revolt of Europe started long before the Renaissance proper. And even in the Renaissance period the anti-Christian intellectual outlook of the free-thinking academies in Italy was partly at least forced on them by the Church, which 'identified the new learning with heresy'. If men had to choose between obscurantism and a freedom of thought which was held to be anti-religious, religion itself compelled them to choose the latter. But the Oxford Reformers, Colet, More, and Erasmus, understood that Christian loyalty admits and even positively demands a candid and unfettered search for truth—following the argument whithersoever it leads. It is in this way alone that every thought can be 'led captive to the service of Christ'.

The architects have shown a more excellent way. And it will be thus in the Great Church of the future. Art and letters, science and education, will all be free in their respective provinces. But all, as actuated by the Christian motive, and drawing their inspiration from God's Spirit, will be recognized and reverenced as functions of the one living Body.

Similarly, Christian Fellowship ought not to mean one more association added to or substituted for our other natural associations. Rather it means these other associations, but with a common sharing in the Christ-life as the source and basis of their unity. The ground of Fellowship is supernatural: but it manifests itself in the natural groupings.

So St. Paul finds in Our Lord's Ascension the supernatural source of Fellowship and of the organic life of the Christian Body. He ascended up on high, and then descended, giving gifts to men—those gifts so various in degree and kind which taken together comprise the Church's life. He that ascended far above all heavens, triumphant through sacrificial love, descended again into this earth below—i. e. in the coming of the Spirit.[1] He that descended on His waiting followers is He that ascended 'that He might fill all things'. He gave some to be apostles, some prophets, some schoolmasters, and some shopkeepers 'for the building up of the Body of Christ'.

We suggested above that the problem of society is

[1] This interpretation follows the true text of Eph. iv. 9, as in R.V.

that of the redirection of the wills and desires of men and women. That is what the Ascension had made possible. The Risen Christ had led captivity captive: He had ascended far above all heavens. So that His Church had not to confront the world merely with the statement of a problem: it carried the final answer in its hands. It went out with a victory behind it. The Master, whose 'way' and whose influence it proclaimed, was enthroned as Sovereign in the Universe. The everlasting doors had been lifted up and the King of Glory had gone in. He held the keys of hell and of death. He had taken on Himself man to deliver him.[1] That is, He had redeemed human life. His Ascension and His coming in the Spirit implanted the fruits of this redemption in the hearts of all who accepted Him. He had come, as He promised, to 'abide in' them. Set free now from the limiting conditions of physical life in the days of His flesh, He was nearer to them than He had been before. He pierced to the innermost core of their very beings, living Himself within their personalities, making them literally new men. He became the very life of their lives, so that all their instincts and desires revolved henceforth round a new Centre. Thus He sent His followers out into the world transfigured and remade, to live the ordinary life, indeed, but to live it as changed and redirected people. Thus the Ascension meant, as St. Paul claims, the irruption into human society of a new and supernatural life, organizing the new Fellowship. It is as individuals appropriate the life of the crucified and ascending Christ that genuine fellowship is made possible. 'Christ in you' is the source of Fellowship. That means a spiritual transformation. It is very far removed from the mere 'behaviour' of man's instinct of gregariousness.

This point we shall work out in our final chapter. Meanwhile, we can see more clearly what is meant by 'the Fellowship of the Holy Spirit'. The Spirit always creates Fellowship: it is the essential function of the Spirit and the surest sign of the Spirit's presence. There

[1] 'Tu ad liberandum suscepturus hominem, non horruisti Virginis uterum.'—The *Te Deum.*

can be no Fellowship without the Spirit, for Fellowship is God in human life. As we look back over Christian history at the most signal comings of the Spirit, whether to small groups or to the Church at large, it seems to be true that one of the first effects has normally been a new consciousness of Fellowship.[1] But the times when the Church has been most strongly actuated by the impulses of mere group-loyalty have not been those in which the Spirit of Christ has been conspicuously present in her. The Roman Church was gregarious enough when it gave its support to the Inquisition, or the English Church when it extruded Wesley. But such acts are the antithesis of fellowship. It would not be easy to find in these phenomena any clear manifestation of the Spirit. This distinction between group-loyalty and fellowship is, I should hold, at bottom the distinction between proselytizing and evangelization.

Thus, so far is it from being true that the operation of the social instinct will necessarily result in wider fellowship, that it often cuts directly across it. Our Lord said He had come into the world to bring not peace but division (διαμερισμόν). Perhaps this is partly what He meant. He broke the ties of mere gregariousness (as expressed in caste, sectarianism, &c.) in order that Fellowship might become possible. He 'broke down the middle-wall of partition'. Churches and the clerical profession need to be constantly on their guard lest they should dignify as Christian Fellowship or as loyalty to Christ's commands actions and attitudes to which Psychology would give another and less complimentary name. The fundamental ground of Fellowship is participation in the Christ-life by individual disciples. The love of God, and the influence of Christ, and the Fellowship created by the Spirit (2 Cor. xiii. 13) are at bottom different names for the same thing.

It is clear, too, why the unity of the Church is necessarily a unity in variety. It is because it comes from the Spirit. It is the common supernatural Life in which all its members share, but appropriated in different ways in accordance with all the differing conditions of time, temperament, and

[1] Cf. Chapter II above.

circumstances. To demand of the Church that, everywhere and always, it should be organized in the same form, and worship in precisely the same fashion, is not merely to ask for something very dull: it is to ask for something which is impossible. For the Spirit always creates fellowship: but equally it creates variety. Variety is ever a sign of life, and uniformity a mark of death. In the story of biological evolution there is one step which has never yet been explained. Certain varieties of species have a survival value and therefore survive. But how do you account for the varieties? We can only say that they are 'spontaneous'—that is to say that somehow 'life' makes them. It appears to be true, at least within certain limits, that the most vigorous breeds and stocks tend to run to most spontaneous variations. Where vitality is most intense there we find the most variety. This is an illuminating analogy. The same law seems to hold in the realm of spirit. Wherever in the history of the Church the Spirit's pressure has been most intense, there the life of the Church has been most varied, least patient of being fettered and incarcerated in the neat syllogisms of uniformity. Life can never be confined by logic. Thus, when it comes to a question of organization, or of discussing the terms of recognition for the many separated Christian bodies as integral parts of the Universal Church, the desire to standardize must be sternly avoided. That would be nothing less than to 'quench the Spirit'. It would make a corpse of a living organism. It is not merely a matter of tolerating, but of actively welcoming and praying for as much variety as possible in the expression of the deeper unity. When the Spirit comes, He comes in 'divers manners' (πολυτρόπως, Heb. i. 1). He gives some to be apostles, some prophets, some evangelists—different experiences and different ministries, each, by 'that which every part supplies' helping to form and sharing the life of the Body—the unity of the Christ-life.

A 'closed' Church is inconceivable, once we have understood what the Church means. For if the Church is indeed the Body of Christ—the Embodiment of Truth, the organic expression of His Spirit—it is something which can never be completed under any conditions known to us as yet. It takes the experience of the whole race to explain the full significance of Christ. And experience, which is continually growing, cannot in the nature of things be a finished book. No branch of the Church, no province of the Fellowship, can claim to have more than a broken arc of Truth. The 'perfect round' is in heaven. It can only be adequately apprehended, the life can only be adequately known, in the completed experience of mankind. But 'mankind' is not a fixed and stable quantity. The meaning of the term grows day by day until our race—this flicker of conscious life between two immeasurable eternities—perishes from the face of our earth. That is to say, the completion can never come under the limitations of time and space. The fulfilment of the Church is not in this world. It is, as St. Paul says, in 'the coming age'.

But unto each one of us was the grace given according to the measure of the gift of Christ. Wherefore he saith,

When he ascended on high, he led captivity captive,
And gave gifts unto men.

(Now this, He ascended, what is it but that he also descended into the lower parts of the earth? He that descended is the same also that ascended far above all the heavens, that he might fill all things.) And he gave some *to be* apostles; and some, prophets; and some, evangelists; and some, pastors and teachers; for the perfecting of the saints, unto the work of ministering, unto the building up of the body of Christ: till we all attain unto the unity of the faith, and of the knowledge of the Son of God, unto a fullgrown man, unto the measure of the stature of the fulness of Christ: that we may be no longer children, tossed to and fro and carried about with every wind of doctrine, by the sleight of men, in craftiness, after the wiles of error; but speaking truth in love, may grow up in all things into him, which is the head, *even* Christ.—Eph. iv. 7–15.

CHAPTER VII

THE FELLOWSHIP OF THE HOLY SPIRIT

'The measure of the stature of the fulness of Christ.'—Eph. iv. 13.

THUS Fellowship is no automatic growth. It is made possible by Christ. We have tried to see it as the consummation of that natural tendency to co-operation, traceable all through the order of the Universe, which is the divine love coming to its fulfilment. In this sense Fellowship comes out of the heart of God. And in this sense, therefore, it is Man's real destiny. In that free co-operation between all persons which is love in its highest activity, man fulfils the deepest need and the inner necessity of his being. The Spirit of God achieves His age-long purpose in the perfecting of Fellowship. If this be so, we must think of the League of Nations not as a final desperate resource for saving man's life from destruction by man's own fury. The 'last hope of civilization' it certainly is, but it is ever so much more than that. It is rather the instrument of a new world-order based upon the certain will of God. In a solemn sense it is a 'new covenant'. It embodies man's belated understanding of the architecture of the Universe and the laws by which human life must be controlled if it is to win enduring freedom. It is a new recognition of God's ways. The possibility of the world-state is rooted in the character of God. It is God's Love in its fullest manifestation under the limitations of finite life.

But all love essentially involves sacrifice. All progress in co-operation, as much between nations as individuals, necessarily involves sacrifice, as the Primate reminded the world at Geneva. Unity is a sacrificial thing. No group can remain at the level of true fellowship if it is content to be a closed system. For there is in genuine fellowship an impulse to be always sharing its life with others. When a group ceases to be 'missionary' it generally ceases to be a fellowship. The Body is one only in proportion as it is continually given to be broken. So that fellowship must 'die' in order to live. Otherwise its own life becomes unhealthy and its own inner unity is imperilled. An intense consciousness of antagonism against some other group may, as in war, stimulate for the time a strong sense of group-unity. But, as we have seen, it weakens again quickly so soon as the strain of conflict is relaxed. It is not lasting, and it is less than fellowship; though undeniably it is consecrated by gloriously sacrificial acts. For that fellowship should consist in opposition to other fragmentary fellowship-groups is plainly enough self-contradictory. Fellowship is by nature inclusive.

The Fellowship of the Christian Society is confessedly, in one of its aspects, comradeship in the Church *militant.* But the enemy against which it is organized is not some other human group. It is rather a world-enlisting enterprise against all which makes genuine fellowship impossible: and this, as the King has recently declared, is the only warfare ultimately worth waging. It is love sacrificing itself to conquer hate.

We must hold, then, that full and enduring Fellowship involves self-giving, and therefore sacrifice. And this fact, too, Christianity asserts, has its roots in the nature of Reality. Fellowship is the life of God in action; and the life of God is a crucified life, ever triumphing through death and passion. God 'commended His love to us', as the familiar New Testament phrase puts it, by the sacrifice of Calvary. The Christ who declared God's way of life for men and called into being the new world-fellowship, has revealed the fullness of life through sacrifice. 'Except a grain of wheat fall into the ground and die it abides alone: if it die, it brings forth much fruit.' Love's triumphs are achieved through crucifixion. And those who hail in our Lord the supreme expression of the Divine Life in human terms will always recognize in His Cross the revelation in our temporal world of an eternal moment in

God's life. God draws mankind into Fellowship through His eternal crucifixion. Here is the final word about the Universe. Behind the certainty of God's will to Fellowship is the guarantee of its possibility in the sacrificial life of God. In the very presence-chamber of the Eternal, where the secrets of the Universe are sealed, is a 'Lamb standing as though it had been slain'. And this is the charter of world-fellowship. The Christian facts are the guarantee that 'multitudes which no man can number' can become 'one' in the fulfilment of God's designs.

This line of thought keeps very close in to St. Paul. It is fundamental in his outlook, and indeed in that of the whole New Testament, that it is the Cross which makes Fellowship possible. The Cross had inaugurated a new Covenant between man and God and between man and man. By the Cross He had slain the enmity. By the Cross those who were 'far off' had been made 'near' in the new Society. By the Cross He had thrown down the dividing-wall. By the Cross He had become 'our Peace'.

We have seen that Fellowship is a costly thing, and Calvary proclaims how much it cost. No less than *that* would avail to fling down the barriers and undermine the old antagonisms. Only Calvary can destroy privilege.

And St. Paul had found this verified in history. The chosen nation of God had been 'rejected' because it had refused its destiny. It should have been a power working for fellowship, and it rested content in its particularism. The tragedy is written across its sacred books. The Old Testament story is the spacious record of God's self-revelation gradually unfolded to mankind. But it also records for us the evolution of a unique social consciousness in response to developing ideas of God.[1] Abraham's family is depicted for us widening out into the nation-state 'as the sand which is by the sea-shore innumerable'. The call to fellowship on a religious basis was an integral part of Israel's vocation. Its group-unity was through and through religious. In this, of course, there is nothing exceptional—it is equally so with any social group. Men's conception of the Deity they worship must affect, if it

[1] See Hamilton, *The People of God*, vol. i, chapters ii and iii.

does not actually control, their social life. But with Israel something had gone wrong. The vocation of Israel was religious genius. Less gifted than the Egyptians, Greeks, or Romans in most departments of civilized life, the Hebrews nevertheless had been given a unique spiritual insight which was their trust on behalf of the human race. Their understanding of the Divine character, learnt in the splendid school of their Saints and Prophets, should have led them out as pioneers in the achievement of world-fellowship. But the prophets prophesied in vain. The development of Jewish religious thought, travelling from the earliest dim cultus of the God who 'broke forth' in the storm on Sinai, to the high spiritual communion with God the holy Father of mankind which we find in the Psalms and at least the later Prophets, is outside the limits of this book to trace. It can be read in countless excellent manuals.[1] But it is clear that it stopped short of its goal. The social organization of the people failed disastrously to keep pace with their growing knowledge of the Divine character. Once they had reached a monotheistic faith—which probably was not long before the Exile—internationalism should have followed. They should then have recognized that the Jewish faith was meant to impart itself to the whole world, to be shared in fellowship with all mankind. But the people stopped short of that recognition. The writer of the missionary pamphlet known in our Bible as the Book of Jonah, and the nameless prophet of the Exile, made their protest unregarded.

It was indubitably the will of God that Israel should be a 'third', along with Egypt and Assyria.[2] It was a 'small thing' that the little people whom Yahweh had made the 'servant' of His purposes should re-evangelize the Jewish remnant. 'I will also give thee for a light to the Gentiles, that thou mayest be my salvation unto the ends of the earth' (Isa. xlix. 6). But this call to new adventure was unrecognized. The people,

[1] Cf. Budde, *The Religion of Israel*; Hamilton, *The People of God*, vol. i; Nairne, *The Faith of the Old Testament*; also in Kent's *Shorter Bible*.

[2] Isa. xix. 23–4.

hammered into intense group-loyalty by the sufferings of the Maccabbean period and the strong hand of their Roman overlords, failed to hear and respond to their vocation. They remained a theocratic nation-state, intensely organized within itself, and seeking at all costs to preserve its 'purity', that is, its religious and social separatism. No doubt, as regards the Jews of the Dispersion this statement demands a certain qualification. There was a considerable propaganda, and the hard conditions of entrance to the society (especially in the matter of circumcision and the observance of the food laws) were being made less rigorous and forbidding.[1] But, on the whole, the Jewish nation-state failed to work out its own destiny. It was self-sufficient and bitterly exclusive. 'Amongst themselves they keep faith inviolable and are always ready to help one another. They hate all the rest of the world as enemies.' So runs the famous account of the Jews in Tacitus.[2] And the scathing words of Christ corroborate it. Their missionary enterprise, He said, was proselytism, not real evangelizing. They were not really sharing Fellowship. 'You compass sea and land to make one proselyte, and when he is made you make him two-fold more the child of hell than yourselves!'

Thus Judaism, failing in its mission, had become a positive obstacle to world-unity. The cleavage between Jew and Gentile cut deeper than most in the ancient world. Only the Crucifixion could annul it.

To make his point St. Paul had recourse to one of his favourite architectural metaphors. The great Temple at Jerusalem ought certainly to have been the symbol of a world united in spiritual Fellowship. God's House—as our Lord said, quoting Isaiah (lvi. 7)—should have been the house of prayer *for all nations*. But the 'great refusal' was built in its very stones.

[1] Lake, *Earlier Epistles*, pp. 23–7.

[2] 'Quia apud ipsos fides obstinata, misericordia in promptu, sed adversus omnes alios hostile odium. Separati epulis discreti cubilibus, proiectissima ad libidinem gens [this is a libel] alienarum concubitu abstinent. . . . Transgressi in morem eorum idem usurpant, nec quidquam prius inbuuntur quam contemnere deos, exuere patriam, parentes liberos fratres vilia habere,' Tac. *Hist.* v. 5.

Between the Court of the Gentiles and the Holy Place a stone-balustrade had been erected bearing inscriptions in several languages which threatened with death any Gentile who should pass it.[1] This barrier, says St. Paul, Christ had thrown down. 'He had broken the middle-wall of partition and abrogated by His flesh the enmity, the law of the commandments consisting in these notices. In this way He had made of the two one.' (Eph. ii. 14, 15.) The gulf between Jew and Gentile was transcended. In Christ Jesus neither circumcision counted anything nor uncircumcision: in Him there could be no distinction: in Him there was neither Jew nor Greek.

That the thing did happen is a fact of history. We have tried in an earlier chapter to make some estimate of the way in which the new Society achieved what the Empire had never succeeded in doing, and gave the world an effective, living unity in which the deepest divisions were transcended. We have studied, too, what its members themselves thought. It is perfectly clear, explain it as we may, that those who were members of the new Israel, partaking in this emancipating Fellowship, believed that all that had happened was caused directly by the death and Resurrection of their Master. This is the whole point of the apostolic writings. It ought, therefore, to prove illuminating and of practical help to our present discontents, if we try to think out a little more exactly how it was that Calvary and Easter had such world-overturning consequences. We must ask what experience, what concrete fact, lies behind these too-familiar phrases. For clearly we are watching the At-one-ment. We are watching the Cross reconciling man with man, as well as sinful man with God's holiness. How did it do this? How will it do it now? It is imperative to face these questions. For if it was the supreme fact of Calvary which destroyed the colour-bar in the ancient world, and brought masters and slaves into honourable partnership, and hallowed the family and ennobled industry, then it is indeed what our stricken

[1] Josephus, *B. I.* v. 5. 2. The Greek version of this inscription has been discovered, and is copied in Armitage Robinson's note on Eph. ii. 14.

world most needs. We Christians know that we possess the secret. But that is of little use unless we share it. And we cannot do that by repeating phrases: we must let the world know what we actually propose, as our serious contribution to harsh problems.

Let us try to make clear to ourselves what really happened.

(i) In the first place, then, the Cross brought new knowledge. It brought the world the enlarging revelation of new conceptions, both of God and Man. It explored depths in the character of God and the possibilities of human nature which otherwise would never have been suspected. In this sense it was, as St. Paul wrote, God's *Wisdom* (1 Cor. i. 24). Calvary showed men unmistakably what was meant by the Fatherhood of God. *Sic Deus dilexit mundum*—so God loved the world. Jesus had drawn picture after picture of God the Seeker after human souls, going forth to find that which was lost, never ceasing the search till He had found it. In His life He had shown men God in action: He came to seek and to save that which was lost. He went about doing good on earth; and in that life men had seen the glory of the only-begotten of the Father. But Calvary was the supreme object-lesson. 'God demonstrated His love to men in that while we were yet sinners Christ has died for us' (Rom. v. 8). Many before Him had spoken about God's love: the prophets of Israel had prayed to Him as 'Father'. But no one had dreamt that *this* was implied in it! It was, and it is still, utterly incredible. Yet once you have seen it, there can be no doubting. This stupendous new revelation of the character of God brought men out into a new atmosphere. It made them free of a world of new values. It could not but involve a complete readjustment of their whole attitude to life. That is to say, it must make men 'change their minds', which is the real meaning of repentance (*metanoia*). After the Crucifixion, Our Lord Himself said, the world could never be the same again. From that time onwards there was the Son of Man seated at the right hand of power. For human life, henceforth, had a different focus.

There had been an irruption into men's experience of certainties unimagined hitherto. What 'the eye had not seen, nor the ear heard, neither had it entered into the heart of man'—*that* was now the central fact of life. The whole world of thought was bound to be revolutionized, and all acknowledged values to be transvalued, by this crucial and decisive new discovery. Men felt that they stood at the gateway of a new age. God had shaken the heavens and the earth by His tremendous utterance at Calvary. 'The old things are passed away: behold they are become new' (2 Cor. v. 17).

This declaration of the Divine Character was clearly the charter of Universalism. For the Cross was a challenge to rethink God: and the whole accepted scheme of things stood condemned in the process. The Spirit 'convicted the world concerning judgement' (John xvi. 8). If God really were 'like that' then the assumptions on which life was built were seen to be morally intolerable. There could not in actual fact be any distinction: the same Lord is rich in mercy unto all them that call upon Him, regardless of status, race, or privilege (Rom. x. 12). Henceforth the idea that any class of people could be regarded as outside the pale became an unendurable blasphemy. The wall of partition was levelled at a blow. It is striking to read how the 'Evangelical revival' with its Gospel centred in the Cross quickly began to recover the same social outlook. 'Evangelical philanthropy overleapt class-barriers, and paved the way for a more searching criticism of class-standards of living.'[1]

For the new conception of the Divine character brought the world an enriched estimate of the worth of human personality. In the light of the Cross man's life was transfigured. It was seen to have eternal significance. The Cross gave a new dignity to the meanest of mankind. It confronted the world with God's valuation. When they looked at the outcast and the serf—a servant of rulers whom kings despised—men knew from the Cross

[1] H. G. Wood in *Property, its Duties and Rights* (Macmillan), chap. vi. See also Malcolm Spencer's admirable book, *The Social Function of the Church* (S. C. M.), especially pp. 61–9.

that '*that* he was worth to God'. Jesus had judged that he was worth dying for. So the Christian mission went to the great capitals where all the scum of the earth flowed together and asserted that it mattered not at all what colour a man's face might be, how degrading his tasks or degraded his position, how rotten and desperate his life—yet, for all that, Christ had died for him. That lifted him to a new self-respect. And it also made other people respect him. It gave a new glory even to social parasites. Most of us find it comparatively easy to love sinners in a sentimental fashion. But it is almost impossible to be even civil to a 'profiteer'. Yet Jesus had chosen one to be His friend. Jesus had died for that horrid little Zacchaeus! He too, then, was entitled to respect. He, too, stood on the same footing of equality.

And this new reverence for personality was bound to penetrate and change all the relationships of the social order. By changing the moral and spiritual relationships in which men and women stood to one another it was bound in the end to change their legal status. 'Rights' in law are the appanage of a legally recognized personality. When the moral recognition had been given, the legal could not be indefinitely delayed. This can be seen in two obvious examples—the status of women and the position of slaves. It is true that St. Paul belongs to the ancient world in his attitude to women. It is also true that the New Testament nowhere directly condemns slavery. Yet in truth it effected a startling revolution in both these provinces of society. Take slavery. The horror of slavery in the imperial world was not that the slave was actively ill-treated. The 'house-slave' in a great family was probably a good deal better off in all that makes for material well-being than the unskilled labourer to-day. The wrongness of it was its degradation of human persons to the level of things. The slave was not recognized as a person. He had no rights before the law. He was bought and sold like a cow or a wheelbarrow, the absolute property of his owner. But as soon as men knew that Christ died for the slave just as much as for his owner, such a relationship was already abrogated. The slave was a person, worth the Cross to God. He was now 'more than a slave, a brother beloved' (Philem. 16). Both he and his master had been 'bought with a price'. They stood in a new moral relationship, and sooner or later it was inevitable that this should define itself in legal changes. In this way, Christianity assisted the evolution of society from 'status to contract', from mere unquestioned privilege to the mutual intercourse of free persons, equal in worth but differing in function.

This 'widened area of common good', including all for whom Christ died in the range of those to whom rights are due and between whom moral obligations hold, profoundly changed the world's standards of social justice.[1] For what is 'just' in a small privileged circle is quickly seen to be actively unjust when a larger circle of rights has to be considered. The extension of the area of justice must inevitably change its content. Henceforth it was not enough to be vaguely 'charitable'. We have to love all other men *as ourselves*. Everybody, that is, must count for one and nobody for more than one. That the New Testament makes entirely clear. And so, with whatever declensions and inconsistencies, the deepest mind of the Church has always held. And this, as we shall see, found its expression in the legal provisions of the Canon Law, which was only repudiated during the Renaissance.

(ii) Secondly, Calvary proved itself 'God's *Power*'. It supplied the expulsive power of a new affection which did actually change men and women and gave a new direction to their wills. The contemplation of the Sacrifice evoked such a passionate love and loyalty as to cleanse men's hearts from their self-centredness and to draw them out in an untiring service for 'even the least of those His brethren'. 'If God so loved us, we ought also to love one another.' Thus those who came under the spell of Christ crucified did experience a new liberation. They were renewed by His transforming spirit and set

[1] Cf. T. H. Green, *Prolegomena to Ethics*, chap. iii, §§ 206–17.

free from the slavery of themselves. The same mind came to be in them which was also in Christ Jesus (Phil. ii. 5). In whatever way we may choose to state the fact, it is plain that the early generations of Christians experienced an immense transforming influence which involved a complete rupture with their past; and that they themselves connected this experience indissolubly with the Cross of Christ. It is hardly too much to say that this transformation was the distinguishing fact about a Christian. To be a Christian, for the New Testament, is to have received the Spirit. And this meant a tumultuous redirection of the whole trend of his desires, a new orientation of his outlook. It meant, in other words, a real conversion. 'If any man be in Christ, there is a new creation' (2 Cor. v. 17).

Here is the real heart of the whole matter. When a man joined the society of Jesus, it was not a question of modifying his habits or of adding on a new habit of Church-going to a course of life which was otherwise unchanged—which is too often what we mean by it. 'You have,' we tend to say to people now, 'various interests and habits. We want you to add one more to your stock. We want you to get the Sunday-morning habit!' But the apostolic age knew well enough that it costs more than that to redeem men's souls. Conversion, for them, meant a moral revolution. It meant a radical redirection of life Christwards, and so towards a full and costly fellowship. It was only by this redirection, achieved by the living Spirit of the Crucified, that Fellowship could become a possibility.

All experience and observation make perfectly clear that this is the root of the problem. All ideal schemes of reconstruction, all the best plans of statesmen and reformers, are wrecked not by the ambitions of a Napoleon, but by the mild yet unshatterable selfishness of the ordinary decent citizen. The problem of Fellowship is psychological—or as Christians prefer to say, spiritual. It all depends upon the change of heart. The spirit of the crucified Jesus, made available by Pentecost, can achieve this for us, and nothing else can. He descended, bringing gifts to men—the gifts that make possible effective unity.

From cover to cover the letters of St. Paul are simply singing this great refrain. He is certain that the hope of a world made new is no impracticable utopianism. For the Christian facts are 'effective guarantees' that the raw material of world-building, that is to say men and women, can rise to new levels of sacrificial service. When the Ascended Christ 'came down into the lower parts of the earth', He came with gifts in His hand. He enriched mankind with new capacities.

The most fatal obstacle to any progress is scepticism about human nature. Mankind will inevitably continue to pitch its expectations low, to be content with tiny ameliorations of the conditions of things as they are, and to close its eyes to the infinite possibilities of a world recreated by the Christ, so long as we acquiesce in a cynical attitude towards the human material available. 'You mustn't expect too much from human nature. This or that scheme may be all very beautiful, but you can't get men and women to rise to it. You must consider the facts of human nature.' So runs the dismal chorus in these years of post-war disillusionment. But this is a fundamental atheism with which the followers of Jesus can never come to any kind of terms. It contradicts the whole purport of His teaching. It contradicts their own most certain experience. Our Lord insisted that people thought so meanly of the possibilities of human nature just because their faith in God was so meagre. He faced the facts: but He faced all the facts. He did not leave God out of His calculations. He knew that for those who would really believe in God—would build their lives upon the axioms on which His own life was built—literally nothing was impossible. The first result of a recovered faith in a Living God, who *does* things, must be a recovered belief in human nature. And Christianity is the only religion which really believes in the man in the third-class carriage. Our politicians to-day distrust the people, because they do not, in their hearts, believe in God as the dominant Factor in human politics. The first condition of effectiveness in any schemes for world-reconstruction is that mankind should re-explore the resources of the Spirit of God. We must learn to believe in men as much as Jesus did.

The writings of the apostolic age—to say nothing of all the subsequent Christian centuries—record that these startling claims in the Lord's teaching had been verified experimentally in the daily lives of quite commonplace people. 'We know it is true because it has happened to us:' that is the burden of the New Testament. The dreary platitude of the worldly-wise, that 'You can't change human nature', is triumphantly refuted by every page of the New Testament writings. The first generation may not have known much philosophy: but they did know what had occurred in their own experience. And they torture language into amazing grammar in their efforts to make clear what had happened to them. They had once, they said, been 'darkness': now they had 'been made light, in the Lord'. They had been crucified with Christ and had been brought to life again with Him. They were 'super-conquerors' (ὑπερνικῶμεν) through Him that loved them. They had been made kings and priests to reign with Christ for ever and ever. They had been 'begotten from God'. 'God, being rich in mercy, for his great love wherewith he loved us, even when we were dead through our trespasses, quickened us together with Christ . . . and raised us up with him, and made us to sit with him in the heavenly places' (Eph. ii. 5–6). Such are some of their stupendous phrases.

It is a profitable exercise with these magnificent assertions still thrilling in our minds to stop and ask ourselves abruptly to what kind of people this language was held to apply. They were a sorry enough company—not altogether unlike Falstaff's fellows. 'Slaves as ragged as Lazarus in his painted cloth when the glutton's dogs licked his sores—and such as indeed were never soldiers, but discarded unjust serving men, younger sons to younger brothers, revolted tapsters and ostlers trade-fallen, the cankers of a calm world and a long peace. You would think I had a hundred and fifty tattered prodigals lately come from swine-feeding.'[1] So their proud commander described his company. And it probably would be no bad description of the first members of the Church of Christ. Not many wise, says St. Paul, not many noble: and not many respectable either, very likely. Many of them were miscellaneous rascals picked up in the dockyards and back streets of notorious ports like Corinth and Alexandria. One would hardly go to Port Said at the present moment to find recruits for a spiritual revival.

No decent religion would have such people about, so the Higher Ethical Thought of the day protested. That 'Christians keep such nasty company' was the refrain of the anti-Christian journalists. A famous paragraph from Celsus gives an excellent insight into this point of view. 'Those who invite people to partake in other solemnities first make the following declaration: He who hath clean hands and sensible speech is to draw near; or, He who is pure from all stain, conscious of no sin in his soul, and living a just and honourable life may approach. . . . But now let us hear what sort of people these Christians invite. "Any one who is a sinner," they say, "or foolish or simple-minded—in short, any unfortunate will be accepted by the Kingdom of God." By "sinner" is meant an unjust person, a thief, a burglar, a poisoner, a sacrilegious man, a robber of corpses. Why, if you wanted an assembly of robbers, these are just the sort of people you would summon.'[2]

'Here,' remarks Harnack, 'Celsus has stated as lucidly as one could desire the cardinal difference between Christianity and ancient religions.' Exactly. The Church knew what the Spirit of Christ could make of them. And it was from men and women of this description that St. Paul quite confidently proposed to build up a regenerated society. For he who has known the transforming power of Christ as an experienced fact in his own life is

[1] 1 *Henry IV*, IV. ii.

[2] Origen (185–254), *c. Celsum*, iii. 59. Quoted from the English translation of Harnack, *Mission and Expansion*, i. 104.

set free from scepticism about 'human nature'. It was St. Paul, who collected these queer people and organized them into the new Fellowship, who understood that the essence of Christianity can best be described as Faith and Hope and Love. This is the sense in which love believeth all things: it knows that no case is a case too hard for God.

This new understanding of human possibility is the basis of the whole Christian social programme. It gives a new meaning to 'personality'; and by so doing it revolutionizes the whole content of morality. 'Justice' and 'rights' take on richer connotations. All moral progress in actual legislation depends upon men's developing conceptions of the value attached to human personality. Justice is, in its classic definition, 'a stable and unvarying will to render every man his due.'[1] But what *is* 'due' to a man? The answer depends upon your estimate of the man's human possibilities. Admit the idea of natural inferiority—of people who are by nature slaves—and you will satisfy the demands of justice if you 'treat them kindly', like your domestic animals. But once you have reached the New Testament point of view, and seen personality as Christ can make it, your ideas of justice will have to be rehandled. 'What is due to a man' means something very different once you come into this larger atmosphere of unrestricted human possibility. Seneca, whose outlook on such questions is fundamentally religious, pleaded that slaves should be thought of as 'humble friends' (humiles amici) and as such entitled to consideration. *Ubi homo est,* he said in another place, *ibi beneficii locus*: every man is an opportunity of doing kind acts. But the Christian standpoint cannot stop short at that: for as Bishop Gore has so strongly pointed out, it is infinitely easier to indulge a half-selfish feeling of benevolence (and miscall it love for our neighbours) than to satisfy the searching demands of justice. 'Love' that is not built upon respect is either lust or weakness of character. And the Christian neighbour-love is the firm will to render unto every man his due, simply in right of

[1] Ulpian, *Digest,* i. 1. 10. Quoted by Dr. A. J. Carlyle in *Property: its Duties and Rights*, p. 124.

the personality which we know that the Spirit of the Lord can make him. Thus what is just includes all that is necessary to the richest and fullest personal development of those to whom the right has been given to be called the 'Sons of God'. It was in this way that the Christian law of charity verified itself in social righteousness. It was in this way that it abrogated privilege and overleapt the mere natural affinities of social and other fragmentary group-loyalties. Men learnt to reverence all, without distinction, 'in Christ Jesus', and Him in all other men and women. Fellowship, as we have seen, is Christ-centred.

Thus the Fellowship of the Holy Spirit was fashioned out of transfigured personalities. And it is inherent in its very nature that it can have no artificial boundaries. It must be as wide as the Spirit's work in man. There is no hope for the bridging of our gulfs except on the basis of a larger reverence, which depends in its turn on a vivid belief in God.

This can be stated in more concrete terms. Practically, it involves the recognition of a higher Court of moral reference over all the enactments of positive state-law and the sharp practice of diplomacy. Europe once had, and has lost, this recognition embodied in actual jurisprudence, and is now beginning to look for it again. It is, at bottom, the law of equity, the Canon Law of the Mediaeval Church, and the only basis of international law. It may be worth while to glance at this development.

The practice of the courts in republican Rome, constantly called upon to decide cases between a Roman citizen and a foreigner—that is to say, between two people who lived under different codes of positive law—evolved the conception of a Law of Nations distinct from and in some senses higher than the state-law of individual states. The Stoics, too, had a similar conception. Their belief in the supra-national City of Zeus—the unity of all mankind in virtue of their common reason—led them to speak about a 'Law of Nature', prior to all law of custom or 'convention', and supplying a higher and more 'natural' standard (nearer, that is, to ideal justice) by reference to which any given law could be judged. The identification of this law of Nature with the law of Nations recognized in the Courts was an inevitable step. It was formally accepted by the jurists 'at least as early as the time of Hadrian'.[1] They were not, in fact, altogether co-extensive. For Slavery was admitted in the law of Nations, and was contrary to the law of Nature. By the law of Nature all men are equal, as the Roman jurists themselves were prepared to admit. But even if there were inconsistences, the foundation had obviously been laid for a far-reaching moralization of jurisprudence. The result of Caracalla's law of citizenship was, in effect, to make the law of Nature the standard code for the whole civilized world. Here there was, then, the formal acknowledgement of rights as vested simply in humanity, irrespective of national or other status. And on this foundation, after the collapse of the spiritual unity of Europe, Grotius tried to rebuild International Law.

But another moral force succeeded Stoicism. The Christian Church developed a suggestion which had been already made by the Stoics themselves, and identified the law of Nature with the revealed law of God. This was the basis of mediaeval Canon law. It would be impossible to overrate the services it rendered to Western civilization. It supplied a court of appeal over princes. In wild times it imposed an effective restraint on the force on which positive law must rely, proclaiming the moral grounds of all law, and delivering the poor from him that was too strong for him by insistence on indestructible human rights. It controlled the idea of the alleged 'rights of property' by continual reference to human need. It even managed to 'restrain the spirit of princes', mitigating the claims of all sectional interests by the higher claim of that moral unity in which alone human life had real significance. It stood supreme over international rivalry. In other words, it confronted a turbulent world with a constant and effective challenge in the name of the Fellowship of the Holy Spirit.

[1] See Bryce, *Studies in History and Jurisprudence*, ii. 135–44, on which this paragraph is based.

The break-up of the mediaeval system involved the repudiation of this law. And half the distresses of our modern world are traceable directly or indirectly to this obliteration of personal rights.

On the one hand, a direct result of it has been the iniquity of our social system. The law of the Church, for example, had recognized no absolute rights in private property. The Roman Law had been based on the assumption of absolute rights (*dominium*) both over property and the lives of other human persons. When the law of the Church was no longer recognized this other legal code stepped in again. It was an incalculable moral set-back. 'It was the Roman pagan conception of absolute property that triumphed at the close of the Middle Ages. This idea, which is the foundation of modern capitalism, led at the time to further attempts to depress the peasants into slavery. It has been fraught with a thousand evils, from which even now the world is slowly and with many struggles trying to recover. The "reception", as it is called, of Roman law, in 1495 in Germany may be taken as the date when the Middle Ages came to an end, and the Roman ideas of property had conquered the West.'[1]

On the other hand, it meant the Balance of Power and all the terrors of international rivalry. It sowed the seeds of August 1914. The political realism of the Renaissance both in individual and state-morality was built upon a radical scepticism. People no longer trusted one another, even in the abstract and as a matter of theory, because they no longer trusted God. The idea of a Fellowship of the Holy Spirit ceased to be a practical force in politics. 'Each for himself and the devil take the hindmost' became the acknowledged code both for men and nations.

The stricken world is beginning to learn its lesson. The nearest approach, in the times in which we live, to the revival of this law of conscience is obviously supplied by the League of Nations. Here we have once again an

[1] Figgis, *Political Aspects of St. Augustine's 'City of God'*, p. 99. Cf. Lindsay, *History of the Reformation*, i. 110 sq., for illustrations.